ALL IS WELL

Daily Inspirational Thoughts

ALL IS WELL

Daily Inspirational Thoughts

ED J. PINEGAR, RICHARD J. ALLEN,
& PAUL A. JENSEN

Covenant Communications, Inc.

Cover image: *Leaving Nauvoo* © Glen Hopkinson
All interior images © Valoy Eaton

Cover design copyrighted 2004 by Covenant Communications, Inc.

Published by Covenant Communications, Inc.
American Fork, Utah

Printed in the United States of America.
First Printing: October 2004

19 18 17 16 15 14 13 12   10 9 8 7 6 5 4 3 2 1

ISBN-13: 978-1-62108-163-0

ABBREVIATIONS

Works frequently cited have been identified by the following abbreviations:

CHFT	*Church History in the Fullness of Times*
CR	Conference Report
CHMR	*Church History and Modern Revelation*
DJJS	*An American Prophet's Record: The Diaries and Journals of Joseph Smith*
DNTC	*Doctrinal New Testament Commentary*
HC	*History of the Church*
TPJS	*Teachings of the Prophet Joseph Smith*

Preface

⌒⁂⌒

This collection of scriptural references, historical vignettes, and inspirational quotes—all pertaining to the restoration of The Church of Jesus Christ of Latter-day Saints in our times—is intended to serve four main purposes: (1) brighten each day of the year with small increments of light and truth; (2) kindle the glow of spiritual awareness and understanding in our lives; (3) foster gratitude to our Father in Heaven for having restored the fullness of the everlasting gospel in our times in the form of the "marvellous work and a wonder" foretold by prophets of old (Isaiah 29:14) and confirmed by the Apostle Peter as the "times of refreshing" coming from the "presence of the Lord" (Acts 3:19); and (4) stimulate prayerful remembrance and application of many of the grand gospel themes and principles that pertain to our covenant commitments.

The prophet Nephi set the theme for a collection such as this when he elucidated with masterful simplicity the plan of salvation as empowered by the Atonement of Jesus Christ. Having passed through the appointed gateway on the basis of faith, repentance, and the purifying baptism by water and by the Holy Ghost, the faithful must then proceed along the strait and narrow pathway by enduring to the end with courage and obedience: "Wherefore, ye must press forward with a steadfastness in Christ, having a perfect brightness of hope, and a love of God and of all men. Wherefore, if ye shall press forward, feasting upon the word of Christ, and endure to the end, behold, thus saith the Father: Ye shall have eternal life" (2 Nephi 31:20).

We sincerely hope this anthology will serve as a daily uplift of spirit and testimony, and as a helpful source of wisdom for lessons, talks, leadership training, gospel study, and family home evening sessions. May we all feast on the word of the Lord more often, gratefully listen to the counsel of our inspired leaders more willingly, and humbly seek to follow God's will with increased conviction and devotion. And may we remember with humble gratitude the valor and sacrifice of the Prophet Joseph Smith and the other founding leaders of the Restoration who gave full devotion—often their very lives—to lay the foundation of this great work. The kingdom of God restored in the latter days is verily the stone "cut out of the mountain without hands" (Daniel 2:45) that was destined to roll forth until it would fill the entire earth in preparation for the return of the Lord in glory and majesty to inaugurate the millennial reign. Let us therefore press forward steadfastly and obediently day-by-day in preparation for that magnificent event.

Ed J. Pinegar
Richard J. Allen
Paul A. Jensen

JANUARY

He giveth power to the faint; and to them that have no might he increaseth strength.

—Isa. 40:29

JANUARY 1
Leadership

Saturday, 1 Jan. 1842: Joseph Smith spends New Year's Day assisted by Bishop Newel K. Whitney and others, stocking the shelves of his just-completed red-brick store in Nauvoo, Illinois (*HC* 4:490). This store would serve the temporal as well as the political, social, and spiritual needs of the Saints in Nauvoo. Like King Benjamin before him, the Prophet practiced the kind of leadership that placed him *among*, rather than *above*, the people. He established his office on the second floor of the store, of which he stated, "In that room I keep my sacred writings, translate ancient records, and receive revelations" (*HC* 5:1). There the Prophet organized the Relief Society on March 17, 1842. The first endowments were given in the upper chamber that spring (on May 4, 1842), prior to the completion of the Nauvoo Temple (*HC* 5:1–2).

"[Jesus] walked and worked with those he was to serve. [His] was not a long-distance leadership. . . . He put himself and his own needs second and ministered to others beyond the call of duty, tirelessly, lovingly, effectively."

(Spencer W. Kimball, *Ensign,* Aug. 1979, 5–6)

JANUARY 2
The Riches of Eternity

Sunday, 2 Jan. 1831: Joseph Smith receives Section 38 at the third conference of the Church, held at Fayette, New York (*HC* 1:140–143). Some of the Saints wondered why the Lord would have them relocate 300 miles west to Ohio during the winter season. The answer is given in the form of a promise: "There I will give unto you my law; and there you shall be endowed with power from on high" (D&C 38:32). This revelation contains many scriptural treasures redirecting the people's focus, including: "if ye are prepared ye shall not fear" (D&C 38:30); "beware of pride, lest ye become as the Nephites of old" (D&C 38:39). Through His prophet, the Lord lays out clearly the great spiritual blessings—"the riches of eternity"—that flow when His people are obedient.

JANUARY 3
Fellowship

Thursday, 3 Jan. 1833: The Prophet Joseph Smith receives the final portion of Section 88, "The Olive Leaf," on this day. The final portion (vv. 127–141) sets forth the order of "the school of the prophets" (v. 127), including a beautiful salutation and covenant of fellowship. These words signal the qualities of fellowship that could well serve as a standard for our relationships with others.

"I believe we members do not have the option to extend the hand of fellowship only to relatives, close friends, certain Church members, and those selected nonmembers who express an interest in the Church. Limiting or withholding our fellowship seems to me to be contrary to the gospel of Jesus Christ. The Savior offered the effects of His atoning sacrifice to all mankind. He said, 'Remember the worth of souls is great in the sight of God' (D&C 18:10). Can we justify doing less?"

(M. Russell Ballard, *Ensign,* Nov. 1988, 28)

JANUARY 4

Education

Wednesday, 4 Jan. 1837: The Kirtland high school meets for an examination in the uppermost level of the Kirtland Temple this day—a testimony that the restored Church was committed to wholesome learning by study and faith (*HC* 2:475). The Lord had previously commanded the Saints to gain knowledge from all disciplines, "That ye may be prepared in all things when I shall send you again to magnify the calling whereunto I have called you, and the mission with which I have commissioned you" (D&C 88:80).

"We find literally hundreds of thousands of our young people holding to the high standards of the gospel. They find happy and uplifting association with those of their own kind. They are improving their minds with education and their skills with discipline, and their influence for good is felt ever more widely."

(Gordon B. Hinckley, *Ensign,* May 2004, 4)

JANUARY 5
Obedience

Wednesday, 5 Jan. 1831: The Prophet Joseph Smith receives D&C Section 39 on behalf of James Covill, a Baptist minister of forty years (see *HC* 1:143–145). Covill had covenanted with the Lord to accept any commandment given him through the Prophet. The revelation confirms that his "heart is now right," but warns him against "pride and the cares of the world" (vv. 8–9). He is commanded to join the Church and promised: "You shall receive my Spirit, and a blessing so great as you never have known" (v. 10). Yet he rejected the Lord's word for "fear of persecution" and "the cares of the world" (D&C 40:2), becoming an early example of how promises can be lost through disobedience.

"The axiom 'You get what you pay for' is true for spiritual rewards as well. You get what you pay for in obedience, in faith in Jesus Christ, in diligent application of the truths that you learn."

(Richard G. Scott, *Ensign,* May 2003, 77)

JANUARY 6
Spiritual Wealth

Friday, 6 Jan. 1837: About this time, the Kirtland Safety Society releases new banknotes into circulation. All goes well for a few weeks until, among other reversals, the enemies of the Church orchestrate a run on the Church-sanctioned bank, which is then (like many other institutions) unable to supply the people with hard currency. The Prophet Joseph Smith later wrote: "At this time the spirit of speculation in lands and property of all kinds, which was so prevalent throughout the whole nation, was taking deep root in the Church . . . in an especial manner to overthrow the Church . . . and make a final end. . . . Many became disaffected toward me as though I were the sole cause of those very evils" (*HC* 2:487–488). Notwithstanding the Prophet's counsel, he is undeservedly blamed for the bank's failure. Many Saints and some leaders apostatize from the Church—a poignant reminder why the Lord has counseled the Saints not to set their hearts upon the riches of the world.

JANUARY 7
Charity

Saturday, 7 Jan. 1836: Due to the high costs associated with building the temple, money and provisions in Kirtland are scarce. In spite of this, "a sumptuous feast" is held at the home of Bishop Newel K. Whitney. Joseph Smith records: "This feast was after the order of the Son of God—the lame, the halt, and blind were invited, according to the instructions of the Savior" (*HC* 2:362). What a fitting example of living according to celestial law. Those who host the poor and needy today will be guests at the Great King's wedding feast tomorrow.

"I reiterate that welfare services is not just a program; it is the gospel in action. . . . It is my desire that we learn from the scriptures and from the counsel of the living prophets and do our part to sustain ourselves, to care for our families, and with generosity and humility to contribute our share to maintaining those less fortunate than we."

(Marion G. Romney, *Ensign,* May 1981, 91)

JANUARY 8
Vigilance

Wednesday, 8 Jan. 1834: Guards are placed to protect the Kirtland Temple as a result of persecution by detractors and the threat of violence at the hands of a gathering mob. Some workmen are seen armed with a hammer in one hand and a rifle in the other (cf. Neh. 4:7–9, 16–18). Of this period, Heber C. Kimball writes in the *Times & Seasons*: "We had to guard ourselves night after night, and for weeks were not permitted to take off our clothes, and were obliged to lay with our fire locks [rifles] in our arms" (*HC* 2:2). Are we prepared to stand up for righteous principles and guard the things of God with our lives as they did?

"I have endeavored all my life to follow one portion of the instructions of the Saviour to his disciples, that is, to 'WATCH.' I am a very watchful man."

(Brigham Young, *Journal of Discourses*, 1:103–104)

JANUARY 9

Sacrifice

Monday, 9 Jan. 1843: Traveling from Nauvoo to Springfield, Illinois, Joseph Smith and his companions stop in Plymouth to visit his brother Samuel and his sister Catherine Smith Salisbury. They enjoy a warm reunion, but Willard Richards records: "While there, my heart was pained to witness a lovely wife, and a sister of Joseph, almost barefoot and four lovely children entirely so in the middle of winter. Ah! thought I, what has not Joseph and his father's family suffered to bring forth the work of the Lord?" (*DJJS, 291*).

"So far as suffering goes I have compared it a great many times . . . to a man wearing an old, worn-out, tattered and dirty coat, and somebody comes along and gives him one that is new, whole and beautiful. This is the comparison I draw when I think of what I have suffered for the Gospel's sake—I have thrown away an old coat and have put on a new one. No man or woman ever heard me tell about suffering."

(Brigham Young, *Discourses of Brigham Young,* 348)

JANUARY 10
Wisdom

Tuesday, 10 Jan. 1832: While laboring diligently on the inspired revision of the Bible, during a period of unusually severe persecution against the Church in Ohio, Joseph Smith and Sidney Rigdon were suddenly called by revelation to go on a special mission (Section 71, dated December 1, 1831) to "confound [their] enemies" (v. 7). This was to dispel antagonism against the Church caused by a series of nine letters written by apostate Ezra Booth and published in the *Ohio Star.* The Prophet comments on their labors ". . . We did much towards allaying the excited feelings" (*HC* 1:241). Forty days later, on this day, January 10, they receive Section 73, in which the Lord instructs them to resume the significant work of translating the Bible. Thus we see how the Lord adapts His tactics with wisdom and prudence in order to accomplish all His designs.

"There are thousands of people that are fighting against us who would, if they knew what we know, lay down their weapons and suppress the spirit to contend against us."

(Lorenzo Snow, *Teachings of Lorenzo Snow,* 176)

JANUARY 11
Integrity

Wednesday, 11 Jan. 1843: Joseph Smith has been falsely charged by his enemies in Missouri. He borrows a carriage from Brother Daniel Russell to convey his companions from Nauvoo to Springfield, Illinois, to stand trial on charges of accessory in the attempted murder of Governor Lilburn W. Boggs. The Prophet is vindicated. On the return trip, the horses bolt while descending a steep hill. The carriage capsizes and falls off the side of a low bridge, causing damage to the carriage but not the riders. Repairs are made. Joseph and Emma later ride out to apologize personally to Brother Russell for the damage caused to his carriage (see *HC* 5:246–248).

"Let us be men of truth, honor and integrity—men that will swear to our own hurt and change not—men whose word will be our everlasting bond. . . . We are trying to raise up a people that shall be men of God . . . men of integrity . . . men who will be fit to associate with the Gods in the eternal worlds."

(John Taylor, *Teachings of Presidents of the Church: John Taylor*, 59)

JANUARY 12
Beware of Greed

Friday, 12 Jan. 1838: The Prophet Joseph Smith had written that 1838 "dawned upon the Church in Kirtland in all the bitterness of the spirit of apostate mobocracy; which continued to rage and grow hotter and hotter" (*HC* 3:1). Warned by a sympathizer, the Prophet escapes this day from the clutches of determined assassins in Kirtland by hiding in a box conveyed out of town on an oxcart. With the mob hot on their heels, he and Sidney Rigdon ride west together toward Missouri. The mob action had been engendered when a number of the leading citizens in Kirtland blamed Joseph Smith for the failure of their business interests—despite the fact that he had repeatedly warned them against unwise land-and-money speculation. Pride and greed supplanted the spiritual element among many of the people for a time, but the kingdom of God would still flourish because of the humility and devotion of faithful Saints.

JANUARY 13
Endurance

Thursday, 13 Jan. 1831: The Church was scarcely six months old when Oliver Cowdery, Peter Whitmer, Jr., Ziba Peterson, and Parley P. Pratt departed from Fayette, New York, on a mission to the Lamanites (in obedience to the Lord's directives in D&C 28 and 30). Now, on January 13, almost three months later, having traveled 1,500 weary miles, having preached many sermons, and baptized 127 converts in Ohio's Western Reserve along the way, they arrive in Independence, Missouri, at "the borders by the Lamanites" (D&C 28:9), and begin preaching to Indians in the unorganized territory. Upon hearing their explanation of the Book of Mormon record, aged Delaware Chief William Anderson responds, "It makes us glad in here," as he places his hand over his heart (*Church History in the Fulness of Times,* 86).

"Patient endurance is to be distinguished from merely being 'acted upon.' Endurance is more than pacing up and down within the cell of our circumstance . . . it is to 'act for ourselves' by magnifying what is allotted to us (see Alma 29:3, 6)."

(Neal A. Maxwell, *Ensign,* May 1990, 33)

JANUARY 14

Order

Thursday, 14 Jan. 1847: Section 136 is given through President Brigham Young at Winter Quarters near Council Bluffs, Iowa, as "The Word and Will of the Lord concerning the Camp of Israel in their journeyings to the West" (D&C 136:1). The Saints are to organize themselves into companies for the trek, "with a covenant and promise to keep all the commandments and statutes of the Lord our God" (D&C 136:2). Special instructions are given to meet the needs of poor people, widows, orphans, and families of those serving in the army. Advance companies are to prepare spring plantings. All is to be done in order, with a spirit of sharing, fellowship, and joyful demeanor, no matter what the circumstances.

"The Lord governs his people . . . in an orderly way through an organization directed by the Lord himself. . . . Under his direction, the First Presidency and the Quorum of the Twelve Apostles provide inspired leadership. What could be more comforting than knowing that a perfect, omnipotent God continually watches over his children in this way?".

(*Ensign*, Apr. 1998, 57)

JANUARY 15
Obedience

Friday, 15 Jan. 1841: The following short notice written by Joseph Smith appears in the *Times & Seasons:* "Elders Orson Hyde and John E. Page are informed that the Lord is not well pleased with them, in consequence of delaying their mission, (John E. Page in particular) and they are requested, by the First Presidency, to hasten their journey towards their destination" (*HC* 4:274). The two fellow Apostles had left in April 1840 on their mission to the Jews in Europe and Palestine (*HC* 4:114). However, Elder Page had lingered in Pennsylvania, so Elder Hyde finally continued on by himself to New York. Elder Hyde, hearing nothing from his companion, continues on alone. After an extremely arduous journey, Elder Hyde will dedicate the Holy Land on October 24. John E. Page later apostatized and was excommunicated on June 26, 1846 (*HC* 7:582).

"President [N. Eldon] Tanner . . . was asked what . . . was the most important attribute of a successful individual or missionary. After a short pause . . . he spoke one word: 'obedience.'"

(Ted E. Brewerton, *Ensign,* May 1981, 68)

JANUARY 16
Sacrifice

Saturday, 16 Jan. 1830: Joseph Smith, Sr., enters into an agreement to give Martin Harris "equal privileges" (i.e., first profits) from the sale of the first edition of the Book of Mormon, then being printed at the E. B. Grandin Printing Company in Palmyra, New York (see *CHFT*, 65). Martin Harris had mortgaged part of his farm to secure the printing costs, and when he grows nervous about this obligation, the Lord admonishes him not to covet his own property, "but impart it freely to the printing of the Book of Mormon, which contains the truth and the word of God" (D&C 19:26). In fact, 151 acres of the Harris farm and house are later sold at auction to satisfy the debt (see *CHFT*, 65–66).

"Let us here observe, that a religion that does not require the sacrifice of all things never has power sufficient to produce the faith necessary unto life and salvation . . ."

(Joseph Smith, *Lectures on Faith* 6:7)

JANUARY 17

Confession

Sunday, 17 Jan. 1836: At Sunday worship services held in the Kirtland "schoolhouse," the time is spent "by the Presidency and Twelve, in speaking each in his turn until they had all spoken" (*HC* 2:376) in what resembles a modern testimony meeting. President Smith adds: "The Lord poured out His Spirit upon us, and the brethren began to confess their faults one to the other, and the congregation was soon overwhelmed in tears, and some of our hearts were too big for utterance." It is instructive to note that this great spiritual feast began with the sincere confession of sins.

"This, of course, does not mean that the people must detail their major sins and crimes, but as has often been heard in testimonies, on fast day and otherwise, when people are speaking they say something like this: 'I recognize my weaknesses and imperfections and I am striving constantly to overcome them and ask you my brothers and sisters to overlook my frailties and errors.'"

(Spencer W. Kimball, *Teachings of Spencer W. Kimball,* 516)

JANUARY 18
Marriage

Thursday, 18 Jan. 1827: Joseph Smith, Jr., and Emma Hale are married this day by a justice of the peace in South Bainbridge, New York. Joseph had met the tall, attractive, dark-haired schoolteacher while boarding at the Hale household near Harmony, Pennsylvania. Because her father objected strongly to the marriage, the couple eloped, and following the ceremony they traveled to the Smith family household in Manchester, New York, to take up residence there. Joseph had come to Harmony as an employee of Josiah Stowell, who was searching for a lost ancient silver mine. Joseph convinced Stowell to abandon the search. Though the mine proved elusive, Joseph found in Emma a treasure of far greater worth (see JS—H 1:56–58; *HC* 1:17).

JANUARY 19
Work for the Dead

Tuesday, 19 Jan. 1841: During the funeral sermon of Col. Seymour Brunson the previous August (1840), Joseph Smith first publicly revealed the practice of baptism for the dead. Now, five months later, the Lord reveals that baptism for the dead is to be performed only in a temple (D&C 124:30). The Lord then commands the Saints to build a temple in Nauvoo with a baptismal font. The first baptisms for the dead were performed properly later that year, on Sunday, November 21 (*HC* 4:454).

"I remember well the first time I read the revelation given through the Prophet Joseph concerning the redemption of the dead—one of the most glorious principles I had ever become acquainted with on earth. To think that I and these Latter-day Saints could go forth into the waters of baptism and redeem . . . those that have gone before us, in the lineage of our father's house, and they come forth and receive a part in the first resurrection!"

(Wilford Woodruff, *Collected Discourses*, 2:209)

JANUARY 20
Relationships

Wednesday, 20 Jan. 1836: The Prophet Joseph Smith performs a wedding ceremony in the evening to unite John F. Boynton (a member of the Quorum of the Twelve Apostles) and Susan Lowell. Many friends, associates, and Church leaders participated in the festivities. The Prophet recounts: ". . . Joy filled every bosom, and the countenances of old and young seemed to bloom alike with cheerfulness and smiles of youth; and an entire unison of feeling seemed to pervade the congregation, and indeed I doubt whether the pages of history can boast of a more splendid and innocent wedding and feast than this, for it was conducted after the order of heaven . . ." (*HC* 2:378).

"I know of no other place where happiness abides more securely than in the home. It is possible to make home a bit of heaven. Indeed, I picture heaven as a continuation of the ideal home."

(David O. McKay, CR, Apr. 1964, 5)

JANUARY 21
God's Mercy

Thursday, 21 Jan. 1836: Upon his brother Alvin's untimely death on November 19, 1823, 17-year-old Joseph was particularly devastated. Realizing that various priesthood ordinances, including baptism, are necessary to obtain exaltation, the family must have been overjoyed with the comforting message in Section 137, which Joseph received this day at the Kirtland Temple. As the Prophet recounts: "The heavens were opened upon us, and I beheld the celestial kingdom of God, and the glory thereof. . . . I saw Father Adam and Abraham; and my father and my mother; my brother Alvin, that has long since slept; And marveled how it was that he had obtained an inheritance in that kingdom, seeing that he had departed this life before the Lord had set his hand to gather Israel the second time . . ." (D&C 137:1, 5–6). Then follow the supernal words (quoted above) that illuminate the way for such as Alvin to obtain salvation (see *HC* 2:380).

"The great vicarious work for our kindred dead in our temples demonstrates both the justice and the fairness of the gospel of Jesus Christ."

(James E. Faust, *Ensign*, Nov. 2003, 54–55)

JANUARY 22
Building the Kingdom

Sunday, 22 Jan. 1843: The Prophet Joseph Smith preaches a sermon at the Nauvoo Temple concerning the building up of the kingdom of God. Some (like the Campbellite sect) were contending that the kingdom of God did not exist prior to the Day of Pentecost, "but I say, in the name of the Lord, that the kingdom of God was set up on the earth from the days of Adam to the present time. Whenever there has been a righteous man on earth unto whom God revealed His word and gave power and authority to administer in His name . . . there is the kingdom of God; . . . Whenever men can find out the will of God and find an administrator legally authorized from God, there is the kingdom of God" (*HC* 5:256–259).

"'Thy kingdom come.' Here an interesting thing happens. By praying that the Lord's Kingdom will be built, we commit ourselves to helping build it. Knowing our own abilities and opportunities, we can confer with God about the ways we—individually and as a church—can help build that kingdom."

(Bernard P. Brockbank, *New Era,* Dec. 1981, 4)

JANUARY 23
Cleanliness

Wednesday, 23 Jan. 1833: In compliance with the Lord's commandment given in D&C 88:74–75, the Prophet Joseph administers the ordinance of the washing of feet for the first time in this dispensation, to members of the School of the Prophets in the nearly completed Kirtland Temple. "By the power of the Holy Ghost I pronounced them all clean from the blood of this generation," he records after he administers the ordinance (*HC* 1:323; cf. 2:287). Some of the symbolism is unmistakable—unless we accept the Savior's cleansing, we have no part with Him (see JST, John 13:8–10). Thus the principles, ordinances, and procedures for making one clean, and therefore worthy to dwell with God, are put in place, line upon line, as an everlasting blessing for the Saints of God.

"The value of moral cleanliness is beyond compare. It cannot be bought by silver or gold, but the price we pay in personal righteousness is of inestimable worth, and will do more to bring about that eternal happiness for which we seek than almost anything else."

(N. Eldon Tanner, *Ensign,* Jul. 1975, 2)

JANUARY 24

Meekness

Sunday, 24 Jan. 1830: About this time, Joseph Smith has an interesting confrontation with one of the most dogged enemies of the Restoration. Under the pseudonym Obediah Dogberry, Abner Cole publishes in his Palmyra newspaper, *The Reflector*, a series of purloined and despoiled excerpts from the Book of Mormon. While setting type at the E. B. Grandin print shop for his own periodical, Cole pilfers several pages of the Book of Mormon where the first edition is being prepared for publication. When Joseph Smith confronts him, Cole wants to decide the issue with a fist fight, but the Prophet persuades him to desist through reason: "'Mr. Cole,' said Joseph, in a low, significant tone, 'there is law, and you will find that out, if you did not know it before; but I shall not fight you, for that will do no good'" (Lucy Mack Smith, *History of Joseph Smith by His Mother*, rev. and enhanced ed., 221). Cole drops his plans, and Joseph demonstrates greatness in not entering a fight he probably could have won to mortal appearances.

JANUARY 25
Priesthood Authority

Wednesday, 25 Jan. 1832: Historically, few details are known about a very important conference that takes place this day at Amherst, Ohio (*HC* 1:243) But the event of crowning importance occurs when Joseph, through the will of the Lord, is sustained and ordained "President of the High Priesthood." In this office he is "to preside over the whole church, and to be like unto Moses—Behold, here is wisdom; yea, to be a seer, a revelator, a translator, and a prophet, having all the gifts of God which he bestows upon the head of the church" (D&C 107:91–92; see also 28:2). As God's mouthpiece on earth, the President of the Church is the only individual authorized to hold and exercise all the keys of the priesthood in their fulness (see D&C 132:7).

JANUARY 26
Scripture Study

Tuesday, 26 Jan. 1836: The Hebrew School in Kirtland is opened under the tutelage of its new instructor, Joshua Seixas, a young Hebrew scholar. Three classes are needed to accommodate the keen interest, Joseph Smith being among the most avid students. He said, "My soul delights in reading the word of the Lord in the original, and I am determined to pursue the study of languages, until I shall become a master of them" (*HC* 2:396). He further said, "It seems as if the Lord opens our minds in a marvelous manner to understand his word in the original language" (*DJJS*, 115). Lorenzo Snow also attends the Hebrew School at the invitation of his sister, Eliza, a recent convert. Lorenzo joins the Church and later becomes its fifth President (see also *CHFT*, 161).

JANUARY 27

Persistance

Monday, 27 Jan. 1840: On Monday, January 13, 1840, Elders John Taylor, Wilford Woodruff, and Theodore Turley walk down the gangplank of the ship that has just brought them from America to serve a mission in England (*HC* 4:76). Now, approximately two weeks later, Elder Taylor is at the home of his wife Leonora's brother, George, and George's wife Ann. Ann informs Elder Taylor that her husband will be back from work later that evening. As he leaves the home, Ann turns to her 13-year-old son George and soberly remarks, "There is a man of God. He has come to bring salvation to our father's house." That young English boy named George Quayle Cannon eventually became an Apostle and a statesman of international renown. Truly we should "be not weary in well-doing" (D&C 64:33), for we cannot know what great things the Lord will make of our humble beginnings and persistent devotion to the cause.

JANUARY 28
Balance

Saturday, 28 Jan. 1843: "Played ball with the brethren a short time. Rode round the city [Nauvoo] with Mr. Taylor, a land agent from New York. Some snow fell" (*HC* 5:260). This entry from Joseph Smith's personal journal illuminates the human side of his personality as a man of varied interests and a balanced nature. He was frequently amused when new acquaintances greeted his robust demeanor, good-natured humor, and boundless energy with surprise, as if somehow a prophet should be anything other than who he was—a man like any other, albeit with a divine calling and mission (cf. *HC* 2:302).

"For a man to be great, he must not dwell on small things, though he may enjoy them."

(Joseph Smith, *HC* 5:298)

JANUARY 29
Political Integrity

Monday, 29 Jan. 1844: It's an election year. The current presidential runners are Martin Van Buren and Henry Clay. Joseph Smith's historian records: "It is morally impossible for this people, in justice to themselves, to vote for the re-election of President Van Buren—a man who criminally neglected his duties as chief magistrate in the cold and unblushing manner which he did, when appealed to for aid in the Missouri difficulties. His heartless reply burns like a firebrand in the breast of every true friend of liberty—'*Your cause is just, but I can do nothing for you.*' As to Mr. Clay, his sentiments and cool contempt of the people's rights are manifested in his reply—'*You had better go to Oregon for redress,*'" (*HC* 6:188). It is under these circumstances, that on this day, in the company of Hyrum and the Twelve, General Joseph Smith, Jr. accepts the nomination by Willard Richards as an independent candidate for President of the United States of America, based on a platform of moral integrity.

"I am confident that so long as we have more politicians than statesmen, we shall have problems."
(Gordon B. Hinckley, *Teachings of Gordon B. Hinckley,* 455)

JANUARY 30
Stewardship

Saturday, 30 Jan. 1841: Joseph Smith enters into his journal for this day: "At a special conference of the Church of Jesus Christ of Latter-day Saints, held at Nauvoo pursuant to public notice, I was unanimously elected sole Trustee-in-Trust for the Church" (*HC* 4:286). In a letter to the county recorder on February 1, he confirms the election and explains that it vested in him (and his successors, as the First Presidency), full powers "to receive, acquire, manage or convey property, real, personal, or mixed, for the sole use and benefit of said Church" (*HC* 4:287). As such, he was not only steward of the revelations given through him (D&C 70:3), but also of the earthly blessings bestowed on the Church. In like manner, we must all be wise stewards over the spiritual and temporal gifts the Lord sees fit to bestow upon us.

JANUARY 31
Good Works

Monday, 31 Jan. 1842: Joseph's journal records: "Assisted in appraising the tithings of Saturday with Emma. Received many calls. Read in the Book of Mormon. After dinner visited Brother Chase who was very sick, and in the evening was in council with Brigham Young, Heber C. Kimball, Orson Pratt, Wilford Woodruff, and Willard Richards concerning Brother Snyder and the printing office; spent the evening very cheerfully, and retired about ten o'clock" (*HC* 4:510). Such is a routine day in the life of a prophet. During His mortal ministry, the Savior told His disciples how to distinguish between true and false prophets: "Wherefore by their fruits ye shall know them" (Matt. 7:20).

"All we ask of any people upon the face of the earth is that they shall judge the Latter-day Saints by Joseph Smith, the prophet of the living God. . . . No man without the inspiration of God, in 14 short years, could have laid the foundation of this great work to which you and I belong."

(Heber J. Grant, CR, Apr. 1920, 12–13)

EBRUARY

The sufferings of this present time are
not worthy to be compared with the
glory which shall be revealed in us.

—ROM. 8:18

FEBRUARY 1
Prayer

Tuesday, 1 Feb. 1831: On or about this day, Joseph Smith meets Newel K. Whitney for the first time. Arriving at the Gilbert & Whitney general store in Kirtland, Joseph greets the astonished proprietor warmly. "'Newel K. Whitney! Thou art the man!' he exclaimed, extending his hand cordially, as if to an old and familiar acquaintance. 'You have the advantage of me,' replied the merchant, as he mechanically took the proffered hand. 'I could not call you by name as you have me.' 'I am Joseph the Prophet,' said the stranger smiling. 'You've prayed me here, now what do you want of me?'" (*HC* 1:146). In a vision in New York, Joseph had seen Newel and his wife Elizabeth—new converts—praying for him to come to Kirtland to give guidance to the growing group of Saints there.

FEBRUARY 2
Missionary Work

Monday, 2 Feb. 1829: Section 4 is given through the Prophet Joseph Smith to his father, Joseph Smith, Sr., on the occasion of a visit to the son's small farm in Harmony, Pennsylvania, some time during the month of February (*HC* 1:28). Although the words are directed to Joseph's father, they apply to anyone with a fervent desire to help build up the kingdom: "O ye that embark in the service of God" (v. 2). Section 4 details the entirety of righteous service in the most economical of terms. Every missionary—indeed, every laborer in the Church—is well advised to commit these words to memory and ponder them frequently as a standard of service in the Lord's kingdom.

"The scriptures are abundantly clear in stating that all members of the Church are responsible to do missionary work. . . . The prophets of this dispensation also have clearly taught the concept that missionary service is the responsibility of all members."

(Spencer W. Kimball, *Ensign,* Oct. 1977, 3)

FEBRUARY 3
Talents

Wednesday, 3 Feb. 1841: The first municipal elections have just taken place at Nauvoo, with John C. Bennett elected mayor. The city council is organized and Mayor Bennett delivers his inaugural address (*HC* 4:288–293). The talented Bennett had been very influential and effective in obtaining a city charter from the Illinois State Legislature and he had gained the confidence and admiration of Joseph and the Saints. Bennett will later resign his office in disgrace (on May 17, 1842; *HC* 5:11–12), losing his position in the Church as well. As long as this man directs his talents toward assisting to build the kingdom, he is capable of good; but when he succumbs to sin and temptation he is notoriously effective—though only temporarily—at heaping persecution upon Joseph and the Church.

"President Joseph F. Smith said, 'Every son and every daughter of God has received some talent, and each will be held to strict account for the use or misuse to which it is put. . . .' The Lord is pleased when we use our talents wisely."

(Joseph F. Smith, *Gospel Principles*, 220–221)

FEBRUARY 4
Citizenship

Thursday, 4 Feb. 1841: The Nauvoo Legion is organized by ordinance of the Nauvoo City Council. Joseph Smith is elected lieutenant-general, with John C. Bennett as major-general (see *HC* 4:295–296). This voluntary organization of independent military men was to adopt "the discipline, drill, uniform, rules, and regulations of the United States army" (*HC* 4:294). At its peak, the Nauvoo Legion numbered some 3,000 men. In effect, it was the civil embodiment of an army of Saints organized to uphold the rights and privileges of citizens under the Constitution (see also *CHFT*, 223).

"It is part of our civic duty to be moral in our conduct toward all people. . . . Citizens should also be practitioners of civic virtue in their conduct toward government. They should be ever willing to fulfill the duties of citizenship. . . . The single word that best describes a fulfillment of the duties of civic virtue is patriotism. Citizens should be patriotic."

(Dallin H. Oaks, *Ensign,* Feb. 1992, 74)

FEBRUARY 5
Light

Monday, 5 Feb. 1844: "I wish you to carry out *my* designs. I have seen in vision the splendid appearance of that building illuminated, and will have it built according to the pattern shown me" (*HC* 6:197). Thus the Prophet Joseph Smith instructs Elder William Weeks, the Nauvoo Temple architect. Brother Joseph had told Elder Weeks he wanted round windows incorporated in the design of the temple. The architect responded that putting round windows in the broad side of a building would violate all known rules of architecture. Joseph insists upon circles, contending that they will be "sufficient to light the whole room" and that "when the whole building [is] thus illuminated, the effect [will] be remarkably grand." Symbolically referring to the eyes as the windows of the body, Jesus Christ instructed His listeners in the Sermon on the Mount: "The light of the body is the eye: if therefore thine eye be single to the glory of God, thy whole body shall be full of light" (JST—Matt. 6:22).

FEBRUARY 6
Listen to the Spirit

Monday, 6 Feb. 1843: The events of this day serve as a reminder of how the Spirit had protected the Prophet Joseph Smith on a related occasion the previous year. On this day, Joseph Smith is reelected mayor of Nauvoo by unanimous vote (see *HC* 5:264–265). When the first mayor, John C. Bennett, resigned on May 17, 1842, amid reports of apostasy and immoral behavior, Joseph Smith was elected mayor in his place (*HC* 5:12–13). A few days previous to that, the Prophet had received, and heeded, whisperings from the Spirit to beware of Bennett's harmful intentions toward him in wanting to place him in danger during a practice battle of the Nauvoo Legion (*HC* 5:3–4).

"I remember when Brother [Harold B.] Lee set me apart as a stake president. He said, 'Listen for the whisperings of the Spirit in the stillness of the night.' Now, I believe in that. . . . and I think I can testify that the Lord has spoken quietly. I didn't hear any words, but in the middle of the night ideas have come into my head which, I think, have been prophetic in their nature."

(Gordon B. Hinckley, *Ensign,* Aug. 2000, 2)

FEBRUARY 7

Liberty

Wednesday, 7 Feb. 1844: Joseph Smith releases his *Views of the Powers and Policy of the Government of the United States,* which outlines his political platform as an independent candidate for the United States presidency. He states, "No honest man can doubt for a moment but the glory of American liberty is on the wane, and that calamity and confusion will sooner or later destroy the peace of the people" (*HC* 6:204). He sets forth a program of positive steps founded in solid Christian principle and common sense, which may wisely be applied even in today's political environment.

"We know, as do no other people, that the Constitution of the United States is inspired—established by men whom the Lord raised up for that very purpose. We cannot—we must not—shirk our sacred responsibility to rise up in defense of our God-given freedom."

(Ezra Taft Benson, *Teachings of Ezra Taft Benson,* 620)

FEBRUARY 8
Family

Wednesday, 8 Feb. 1843: From the Prophet Joseph Smith's journal for this day: "This morning, I read German and visited with a brother and sister from Michigan, who thought that 'a prophet is always a prophet'; but I told them that a prophet was a prophet only when he was acting as such." As if to illustrate the balance and the varied dimensions of his life, he adds later on: "At four in the afternoon, I went out with my little Frederick [his son], to exercise myself by sliding on the ice." The image of Joseph Smith enjoying winter play with his boy is a choice reminder that the Prophet of God was also tending to his vital role as father (see *HC* 5:265).

"Let your family come first. Hold worthwhile family home evenings. . . . Cherish and nurture family members and never allow busy schedules and frustrations to drive a wedge between you and your loved ones."

(Joseph B. Wirthlin, *Ensign,* Nov. 2003, 81)

FEBRUARY 9
Discernment

Thursday, 9 Feb. 1843: Joseph Smith writes the following recollection: "A man came to me in Kirtland, and told me he had seen an angel, and described his dress. I told him he had seen no angel, and that there was no such dress in heaven. He grew mad, and went into the street and commanded fire to come down out of heaven to consume me. I laughed at him, and said, You are one of Baal's prophets; your God does not hear you; jump up and cut yourself: and he commanded fire from heaven to consume my house" (*HC* 6:267–268). Naturally, the catastrophe did not happen. On this same occasion the Prophet reveals what he calls "three grand keys whereby you may know whether any administration is from God." These instructions now comprise Section 129.

FEBRUARY 10
Nurture

Wednesday, 10 Feb. 1836: Joseph's brother Hyrum is hurt: "I immediately repaired to his house and found him badly wounded in his left arm. [H]e had fallen on his axe, which caused a wound about four or five inches in length. Doctor Williams sewed it up and dressed it, and I feel to thank God that it is no worse, and I ask my Heavenly Father in the name of Jesus Christ to heal my brother Hyrum, and bless my father's family, one and all, with peace and plenty, and eternal life" (*HC* 2:393–394). In this situation, as in so many others concerning members of his family, the Prophet Joseph displays a special spirit of concern, compassion, service, and abiding love.

"As a parent, one of the greatest gifts you can give a son or daughter is to consistently nurture a growing testimony of truth, patiently nurturing each child's spiritual capacity. Carefully explain the doctrines of the Church and the power they give when well lived. That foundation will equip a child to resist evil in the world."

(Richard G. Scott, *Ensign,* Nov. 2003, 42)

FEBRUARY 11
Leadership

Saturday, 11 Feb. 1843: During his inaugural speech launching his second term as mayor of Nauvoo, Joseph urges the city council to pursue a course "relieving the city from all unnecessary expenses and burdens, and not attempt to improve the city, but enact such ordinances as would promote peace and good order; and the people would improve the city" (*HC* 5:270). Brigham Young adopted this divine principle of government, having first seen it in Joseph's administration: "I have had some people ask me how I manage and control the people. I do it by telling them the truth and letting them do just as they have a mind to" (*Discourses of Brigham Young*, 355). In the premortal existence, the Savior united His voice with the Father in urging righteous living while maintaining the precious freedom to choose.

"The most advanced, universal, and practical leadership philosophy ever put forth was given in this simple statement by the Prophet Joseph Smith: 'I teach the people correct principles and they govern themselves' (quoted by John Taylor in *Journal of Discourses,* 10:57–58)."

(M. Russell Ballard, *Counseling with Our Councils,* 58)

FEBRUARY 12
Preparedness

Sunday, 12 Feb. 1843: Joseph Smith is visited by a group of respectful young men. He answers their inquiry about the teachings of William Miller, an American zealot who claimed the millennial reign of Christ would begin on April 3, 1843. The Prophet explains that Miller was not so much to blame for his error as the translators of the Bible upon whom he was depending. "I told them the prophecies must all be fulfilled; the sun must be darkened and the moon turned into blood, and many more things take place before Christ would come" (*HC* 5:272). The lesson is clear: we should live each day with devotion, spiritually well prepared—as if it were our last—and not worry about the specifics of when the Lord will return to inaugurate His millennial reign.

"If we knew that we would meet the Lord tomorrow—through our premature death or through His unexpected coming—what would we do today? What confessions would we make? What practices would we discontinue? What accounts would we settle? What forgivenesses would we extend? What testimonies would we bear? If we would do those things then, why not now?"

(Dallin H. Oaks, *Ensign,* May 2004, 9)

FEBRUARY 13
Pride

Wednesday, 13 Feb. 1833: What causes the seeds of pride and apostasy to germinate? Burr Riggs was a man with everything going his way—young, energetic, handsome, and an early convert to, and missionary for, the Church. In October 1831, at the age of 20, he was ordained a High Priest and appointed by revelation to serve a mission to the "south country" with Brother Major N. Ashley (D&C 75:17), a calling he apparently neglected. On the current day, February 13, 1833, a council of High Priests convenes in Kirtland to investigate charges against Brother Riggs, who is "accused of failing to magnify his calling as High Priest, and had been guilty of neglect of duty, of abusing the Elders, and of treating their admonitions with contempt" (*HC* 1:327). On February 26th, he is excommunicated (*HC* 1:327). After sincere repentance he is admitted back into the Church and serves with the faithful on the march of Zion's Camp (*HC* 2:184). Later, he becomes estranged once more from the Church—this time for good.

FEBRUARY 14
Witness

❧❧❧❧❧❧❧

Saturday, 14 Feb. 1835: Acting under authority of the First Presidency, the Three Witnesses to the Book of Mormon (Oliver Cowdery, David Whitmer, and Martin Harris) begin selecting the Twelve Apostles at a special conference in Kirtland. Included are Thomas Marsh, Brigham Young, Heber C. Kimball, Orson Hyde, and the brothers Pratt (Orson and Parley). They have a unique calling: "The twelve traveling councilors are called to be the Twelve Apostles, or special witnesses of the name of Christ in all the world" (D&C 107:23) who are to "build up the church, and regulate all the affairs of the same in all nations" (v. 33).

"We serve as witnesses of Jesus Christ through our baptism, our membership in his Church, our partaking of the sacrament, and our prayers and other actions in his name. But our duty to be witnesses of Jesus Christ requires more than this, and I fear that some of us fall short. Latter-day Saints can become so preoccupied with our own agendas that we can forget to witness and testify of Christ."

(Dallin H. Oaks, *Ensign,* Nov. 1990, 29–30)

FEBRUARY 15
The Priesthood

Sunday, 15 Feb. 1835: Ordinations to the apostleship continue, Lyman E. Johnson, Brigham Young, and Heber C. Kimball having been inducted into the Quorum of the Twelve the day before. Six more join these presiding brethren: Orson Hyde, David Patten, Luke S. Johnson, William E. McLellin, John F. Boynton, and William Smith. Presumably all are ordained by the Three Witnesses as directed by the First Presidency. Parley P. Pratt, Thomas B. Marsh, and Orson Pratt are absent on missions at this time and will be ordained in the next few weeks as they return to Kirtland (see *HC* 2:189–191).

"With these respective quorums in place, we have established a pattern under which the Church may grow to any size with an organization of Area Presidencies and Area Authority Seventies, chosen and working across the world according to need. Now, the Lord is watching over His kingdom. He is inspiring its leadership to care for its ever-growing membership."

(Gordon B. Hinckley, *Ensign,* May 1997, 4)

FEBRUARY 16
Testimony

Thursday, 16 Feb. 1832: Section 76, magnificent in its scope of illuminating the concept of "heaven" in the eternal plan of salvation, is given this day through the Prophet Joseph Smith and Sidney Rigdon. Some dozen or so men are in the room while this vision is opened to Joseph and Sidney concerning the three degrees of glory. The supernal majesty of this sweeping revelation caused the Prophet to suggest "that every honest man is constrained to exclaim *'It came from God'*" (HC 1:252–253).

"Having such a testimony is vital. But of even greater importance is being valiant in our testimony. A testimony of Jesus means that we accept the divine mission of Jesus Christ, embrace His gospel, and do His works. It also means we accept the prophetic mission of Joseph Smith and his successors and follow their counsel. As Jesus said, 'Whether by mine own voice or by the voice of my servants, it is the same' (D&C 1:38)."

(Ezra Taft Benson, *Ensign*, Feb. 1987, 2)

FEBRUARY 17
Harmony

Monday, 17 Feb. 1834: In Kirtland, Joseph Smith organizes the first High Council of the Church. Minutes of the meeting are recorded by Oliver Cowdery and Orson Hyde, corrected by the Prophet, and unanimously adopted by the council as a constitution to that body, then and in the future. These are included in the Doctrine & Covenants as Section 102. The Prophet adds these comments, which are still instructive: "I urged the necessity of prayer, that the Spirit might be given, that the things of the Spirit might be judged thereby, because the carnal mind cannot discern the things of God" (*HC* 2:31). This original High Council was a prototype for the more localized stake high councils used in the Church today.

"And every decision made by either of these quorums must be by the unanimous voice of the same . . . . The decisions of these quorums, or either of them, are to be made in all righteousness, in holiness, and lowliness of heart, meekness and long suffering, and in faith, and virtue, and knowledge, temperance, patience, godliness, brotherly kindness and charity . . ."

(D&C 107:27, 30)

FEBRUARY 18
Scripture Study

Monday, 18 Feb. 1828: Sometime during the month of February, Martin Harris presents a selection of characters copied from the golden plates to Charles Anthon of Columbia College in New York City (see JS—H 1:63–65). Among the leading classical scholars of his day, Professor Anthon attests to the authenticity of the characters and the correctness of Joseph Smith's translation. However, upon learning that the plates were of divine origin and sealed from his view, he withdraws his certification, saying, "I cannot read a sealed book." This event is a remarkable fulfillment of the prophecy in Isaiah 29:11–12 (clarified in 2 Ne. 27:15–20). Martin Harris is confirmed in his support of the Prophet and pledges his assets to underwrite the publication of the Book of Mormon.

"The test for understanding this sacred book is preeminently spiritual. . . . There is no way that an unlearned young frontiersman could have fabricated the great truths contained in the book, generated its great spiritual power, or falsified the testimony of Christ that it contains."

(James E. Faust, *Ensign,* Jan. 2004, 5)

FEBRUARY 19
Missionary Work

Sunday, 19 Feb. 1843: On this cool February day, Elder William Henshaw, on missionary assignment from Lorenzo Snow, leads William Rees Davis, Mrs. Davis, and two of their sons, one at a time, down into the waters of baptism in Pen y Darren, near Merthyr-Tydvil, South Wales (see *HC* 5:281–282). He continues preaching the restored gospel publicly in the Davis home, where a branch of the Church is soon organized. Elder Henshaw presently ordains Brother Davis a priest, after which Brother Davis begins preaching the gospel to his fellow countrymen in their own language (see *HC* 5:312).

"Each of us has a solemn obligation to, first, understand by the Spirit what President Kimball has said over the last decade about the mission of the Church; second, to catch his prophetic vision of missionary work; and third, to implement completely in our own lives the words of our living prophet pertaining to missionary work."

(Ezra Taft Benson, *Ensign,* July 1985, 6)

FEBRUARY 20
Peacemaking

Monday, 20 Feb. 1843: While Joseph Smith is presiding over legal cases presented before the mayor's court, he notices two boys fighting in the street near Mill's Tavern. "I left the business of the court, ran over immediately, caught one of the boys (who had begun the fight with clubs,) and then the other; and, after giving them proper instruction, I gave the bystanders a lecture for not interfering in such cases, and told them to quell all disturbances in the street at the first onset" (*HC* 5:282).

"Have you ever wondered how you can be a peacemaker? Really, our opportunities are unlimited. . . . We can pray together for the spirit of peace. We can be a peacemaker by avoiding criticism. . . .We can be a peacemaker by practicing and teaching forgiveness. Jesus was asked how many times one should be forgiven, and he replied that we should forgive without limit. Forgive him 'seventy times seven' (Matt. 18:22)."

(Franklin D. Richards, *Ensign,* Nov. 1974, 106)

FEBRUARY 21
Obedience

Wednesday, 21 Feb. 1844: During a sermon given in the assembly room at Nauvoo in the evening, Joseph Smith instructs the people, "showing them that to get salvation we must not only do some things, but everything which God has commanded" (*HC* 6:223). After Christ's 40-day fast in the wilderness, the devil tried to tempt Him to satisfy His hunger by commanding stones to be made into bread. To this Jesus responded, "It is written, Man shall not live by bread alone, but by every word that proceedeth out of the mouth of God" (Matt. 4:4).

"Our unquestioning obedience to the Lord's commandments is not blind obedience. President Boyd K. Packer in the April conference of 1983 taught us about this: . . . 'We are not obedient because we are blind, we are obedient because we can see.' . . . We might call this 'faith obedience.'. . .'Faith obedience' is a matter of trust. The question is simple: Do we trust our Heavenly Father? Do we trust our prophets?"

(R. Conrad Schultz, *Ensign,* May 2002, 30)

Tuesday, 22 Feb. 1842: During the month of February 1842 (and into March), the Prophet Joseph Smith is working on a translation "from the Records of Abraham" (*HC* 4:548) as contained in ancient rolls of Egyptian papyrus obtained in 1835 (*HC* 2:348–351). The initial excerpts were published in two issues of the *Times & Seasons* (March 1 and March 15, 1842) and later incorporated into the Pearl of Great Price (see *HC* 4:520–534). The restoration of the gospel brought with it a flood of new scripture of priceless value.

"I can't understand why those of other faiths cannot accept the Book of Mormon. One would think that they would be looking for additional witnesses to the great and solemn truths of the Bible. . . . God be thanked for this precious and wonderful testimony. Let us read it. Let us dwell upon its truths. Let us learn its message and be blessed accordingly."

(Gordon B. Hinckley, *Ensign,* Jun. 2000, 18–19)

FEBRUARY 23

God's Laws

Wednesday, 23 Feb. 1831: As it now stands, Section 42—"embracing the law of the Church," as Joseph Smith expressed it (*HC* 1:148)—was revealed in Kirtland in two parts: verses 1–73 were received on February 9, 1831, and verses 74–93 were given on this day. In this important revelation, God proclaims numerous laws to help perfect the Saints and prepare them to be "gathered in one, that ye may be my people and I will be your God" (D&C 42:9). These commandments include "dos and don'ts" of saintly behavior, plus other instruction pertaining to Church organization.

"Altogether this [Section 42] was a most important revelation. . . . Faithful men and women were greatly delighted at being members of a Church which the Lord acknowledged as His own, and to which He communicated His word through His inspired Prophet as He did at this time."

(Gordon B. Hinckley, *Doctrine and Covenants Student Manual*, 82)

FEBRUARY 24
Victory

Monday, 24 Feb. 1834: Section 103 is given at Kirtland this day in response to an urgent report about the trials and dislocations suffered by the Saints in Missouri. The Lord states the principles by which Zion is to be redeemed: (1) strict obedience to His commandments, (2) dependence upon His power, (3) leadership—specifically the leadership of the Prophet in organizing and commanding companies of troops to come to the aid of the Saints (later known as "Zion's Camp"), and (4) willing sacrifice. The Lord explains that He allows this tribulation to continue so that the enemies of the Church "might fill up the measure of their iniquities" (v. 3), and the Saints "might be chastened for a little season" (v. 4), until they learn to follow the Lord's counsel (see D&C 105:6).

"I have had more sorrow over one apostate in this Church than I have in attending the funerals of all the patriarchs and prophets and Latter-day Saints that I ever followed to the grave; because when I see men and women die who have been faithful I know they have gained a victory."

(Wilford Woodruff, *Collected Discourses*, 3:83–84)

FEBRUARY 25
Prophecy

Sunday, 25 Feb. 1844: Reports of renewed violence are heard from Missouri and closer to home from detractors like Thomas Sharp, editor of the *Warsaw Signal,* while apostasy festers in Nauvoo from men previously loyal and honored. Joseph once told his audience that when he was discouraged or afflicted, he would prophesy deliverance. So on this rainy, foggy evening in 1844, with a clear awareness of the dangers facing the Church evidenced in new threats of extermination, Joseph prophesies at a prayer meeting "that within five years we should be out of the power of our old enemies, whether they were apostates or of the world" *(HC* 6:225). Joseph and Hyrum certainly passed "out of the power" of their enemies, and the Church was nestled safely in the valleys of the everlasting hills.

"Now if we understand the words of Peter when he said, 'We have also a more sure word of prophecy' (2 Pet. 1:19), then in other words, there isn't any other way in this world that we can know the mind and the will of the Lord as intelligently and assuredly as we can know it through the holy prophets."

(LeGrand Richards, *Ensign,* Nov. 1975, 50)

FEBRUARY 26

Parents

Sunday, 26 Feb. 1843: Joseph Smith remains at home all day with his widowed mother, who is sick with a lung infection. "I nursed her with my own hands" (*HC* 5:290). Beset with a heavy load of duties, he chooses instead to attend his 68-year-old mother. Lucy Mack Smith had miraculously survived a battle with tuberculosis in her mid-twenties—a malady that had taken the lives of her two older sisters, Lovisa and Lovina. Throughout his days, the Prophet Joseph Smith treated his parents with the utmost affection and consideration. Following his martyrdom, Lucy Mack Smith spent her final years with Emma.

"The commandment to honor our parents has strands that run through the entire fabric of the gospel. It is inherent in our relationship to God our Father. It embraces the divine destiny of the children of God. . . . The commandment to honor our parents echoes the sacred spirit of family relationships in which—at their best—we have sublime expressions of heavenly love and care for one another."

(Dallin H. Oaks, *Ensign,* May 1991, 15)

FEBRUARY 27
Health

Wednesday, 27 Feb. 1833: Most Church members are familiar with the circumstances surrounding the coming forth of the revelation known as the Word of Wisdom (D&C 89) and of the small room used by the brethren attending the School of the Prophets above Bishop Whitney's general store in Kirtland. We recall that Joseph entered the smoke-filled room, noting with dismay the conditions that were causing eye and lung irritation; and how Emma spent hours cleaning up tobacco juice from the floor. But the real value of this conflict resolution is found in the treasures of wisdom comprising the revelation itself.

FEBRUARY 28
Freedom from Debt

❧

Monday, 28 Feb. 1842: The Prophet Joseph Smith, acting as Trustee-in-Trust for the Church, pays $2,700 to Robert Pierce, which is the balance owed this man for the purchase of his farm in Pennsylvania. Mr. Pierce issues a statement of satisfaction: ". . . Many supposed, or pretended to suppose, I would get nothing in return; but I wish to say to all my old friends and enemies in Pennsylvania . . . that I have received my pay in full from the Church of Jesus Christ of Latter-day Saints. . . ." *(HC* 4:519). The Church, from the time of its inception, has cultivated a strict policy of paying off its debts, even when its enemies thought nothing of seizing or destroying property.

"Some debt—such as for a modest home, expenses for education, perhaps for a needed first car—may be necessary. But never should we enter into financial bondage through consumer debt without carefully weighing the costs. . . . We are a people of integrity. We believe in honoring our debts and being honest in our dealings with our fellow men."

(Joseph B. Wirthlin, *Ensign,* May 2004, 41–42)

MARCH

*Wherefore, lift up your hearts
and rejoice . . . that ye may be able
to stand.*

—D&C 27:15

MARCH 1
Perseverance

Thursday, 1 Mar. 1842: It is a very busy day for the Prophet. This morning he commences publishing his translation of the Book of Abraham in the *Times & Seasons*, along with a lengthy letter he wrote to John Wentworth, editor of the *Chicago Democrat*, giving a "sketch of the rise, progress, persecution, and faith of the Latter-day Saints, of which I have the honor, under God, of being the founder" (*HC* 4:535). Included in the letter is an account of many of the events of early Church history, including Joseph's First Vision, the coming forth of the Book of Mormon, and thirteen articles of faith—a comprehesive summary of the Church's basic beliefs and principles. This is one day of many representing the toil and forward progress of the early Saints.

"*Perseverance* means to continue in a given course until we have reached a goal or objective, regardless of obstacles, opposition, and other counterinfluences. . . . Perseverance is a positive, active characteristic. . . . It gives us hope by helping us realize that the righteous suffer no failure except in giving up and no longer trying."

(Joseph B. Wirthlin, *Ensign,* Nov. 1987, 8)

MARCH 2
Honesty in Financial Matters

Wednesday, 2 Mar. 1842: Joseph Smith pays to the tax collector, Walter Bagby, the state and county taxes due, but refuses to pay city taxes for Commerce, "as the demand was illegal, there being no such place known in law, the city and town of Commerce having been included in the city plat of Nauvoo, but continued by our enemies on the tax list for the purpose of getting more money from the Saints" (*HC* 4:542). Later, Joseph Smith draws attention to this man's "oppression, injustice, and rascality" (*HC* 6:4).

"The Lord also expects us to perform our financial duties to Him and others in an honest manner. This means an honest day's work for our daily wages. . . . It means that we treat people who work for us fairly in every instance. And it means we are honest in the payment of our taxes. We must also be honest with the Lord, for a man can rob God (see Mal. 3:8). . . . Meeting these financial obligations is a requirement for all those who desire to enter the temples of God."

(William R. Bradford, *Ensign,* Feb. 2003, 52)

MARCH 3
Liberty Through Truth

Sunday, 3 Mar. 1839: Joseph Smith and his companions attempt to escape from illegal imprisonment. They were cast into "Liberty" Jail after a mock trial. Knowing they were being illegally detained, they made three escape attempts—the first on February 7 (see *HC* 3:257), and the second attempt on this day. In somewhat humorous undertones, Joseph writes the Saints of the attempt: "We should have . . . escaped the mob . . . but unfortunately for us, the timber of the wall being very hard, our auger handles gave out, and hindered us longer than we expected . . . and before we could fully succeed, our plan was discovered; we had everything in readiness, but the last stone . . ." (*HC* 3:292).

"The dungeon had inner and outer walls which, combined, were four feet thick. Loose rocks were placed between the walls to thwart any attempt at burrowing through. Unjustly arrested and unjustly confined, Joseph and his companions tried twice to escape but failed. As thick as those walls and that door were, and as securely as they kept the Prophet and his fellow prisoners in, the walls were not thick enough to keep revelation out!"

(Neal A. Maxwell, *Ensign,* Aug. 1986, 11)

MARCH 4
Constitutional Rights

Wednesday, 4 Mar. 1840: Joseph Smith arrives back in Nauvoo after his journey to petition President Martin Van Buren for redress of the wrongs of the Saints. He comments, in regard to the president's (and Congress') refusal to provide assistance: "I discovered that popular clamor and personal aggrandizement were the ruling principles of those in authority; . . . And may he [Van Buren] never be elected again to any office of trust or power, by which he may abuse the innocent and let the guilty go free" (*HC* 4:89). In fact, Van Buren was defeated in the presidential election of 1840, and again in 1848. The Saints resolved, upon the Prophet's return, to appeal their case to "the Court of Heaven" (*HC* 4:108).

"I reverence the Constitution of the United States as a sacred document. . . . I testify that the God of heaven sent some of His choicest spirits to lay the foundation of this government, and He has now sent other choice spirits to help preserve it."

(Ezra Taft Benson, *Ensign,* Nov. 1987, 7)

MARCH 5
Sacrifice

Saturday, 5 Mar. 1836: For the past three years, much of the efforts of the Saints in Kirtland has been directed toward building the temple—all at significant sacrifice. As we read in Church history how Joseph Smith and others toiled in the rock quarry at Kirtland, cutting and hauling stone for the temple, or how the women pulverized their fine china to mix with the plaster for the temple so the exterior would sparkle and illuminate the reflected light of the finished edifice, are we willing to sacrifice so unselfishly as did our forebears? Today, Joseph records: "In the afternoon the board kiln took fire, and the lumber was principally consumed. To the best of my recollection this is the fifth or sixth time it has burned this winter" (*HC* 2:405). These faithful laborers had to endure such disappointments as fires, illness, danger from hostile enemies, and inclement weather. Yet still they endured, and through their sacrifice built a holy temple unto our God.

MARCH 6
Prayer

Saturday, 6 Mar. 1841: Section 125 is given in response to an inquiry of the Prophet Joseph Smith on behalf of the Saints who fled from Missouri and settled in the Iowa Territory across the river from Nauvoo. In this revelation, the Lord commands the Saints to "gather themselves together unto the places which I shall appoint unto them by my servant Joseph, and build up cities unto my name, that they may be prepared for that which is in store for a time to come" (v. 2). This last is evidently a reference to the coming exodus to the Rocky Mountains. Thus the Lord gives an answer to a humble and sincere prayer.

"Every problem that afflicts humankind can be solved if we can only talk to the Lord and then listen when the Lord answers, which is equally important."

(Harold B. Lee, *The Teachings of Harold B. Lee,* 419)

MARCH 7

Preservation

Monday, 7 Mar. 1831: Section 45, with its comforting message, is received. The Saints in New York had been commanded to unite with the expanding Church in Ohio (see D&C 37:3). In response to this call, Joseph and Emma arrived there about the first of February. Joseph recalled: "At this age of the Church many false reports, lies, and foolish stories, were published in the newspapers, and circulated in every direction, to prevent people from investigating the work, or embracing the faith" (*HC* 1:158). Seeking guidance, he inquired of the Lord, and received Section 45. The Saints are promised that if they will "stand in holy places" (D&C 45:32) and take "the Holy Spirit for their guide" (v. 57) they will be empowered to establish a "New Jerusalem" (v. 66).

> Let the Holy Spirit guide;
> Let him teach us what is true.
> He will testify of Christ,
> Light our minds with heaven's view.
>
> (see *Hymns,* no. 143 for full text)

MARCH 8
Record Keeping

Tuesday, 8 Mar. 1831: Section 47 is given, calling John Whitmer to succeed Oliver Cowdery as scribe and historian for the Church. The Prophet later explained one of the key reasons for keeping careful records: "If you assemble from time to time, and proceed to discuss important questions, and pass decisions upon the same, and fail to note them down, by and by you will be driven to straits from which you will not be able to extricate yourselves, because you may be in a situation not to bring your faith to bear with sufficient perfection or power to obtain the desired information; or, perhaps, for neglecting to write these things when God had revealed them, not esteeming them of sufficient worth, the Spirit may withdraw and God may be angry; and there is, or was, a vast knowledge, of infinite importance, which is now lost" (*HC* 2:199).

"If history is not accurate, it is harmful. . . . We have a very good system of keeping records in the Church, and it is because of the commandments which have been given us by the Lord."

(Joseph Fielding Smith, *Doctrines of Salvation,* 2:198, 203)

MARCH 9
Death is Not the End

Saturday, 9 Mar. 1844: In the city of Nauvoo, 57-year-old Brother King Follett is working deep in a well, laboring to rock up the inside wall. Suddenly a rope breaks and a heavy bucket of rocks being lowered down to Brother Follett falls, killing him. He had been a true and faithful member since he first heard the gospel preached in the spring of 1831. He will be buried tomorrow with Masonic honors. Next month during April conference, Joseph Smith will deliver his funeral eulogy—the most eloquent and best known of the many he gave. The King Follett discourse reveals profoundly comforting truths about the character of God and man's relationship to his Creator (*HC* 6:248–254; see also April 7).

"What a wonderful thing is death, really, when all is said and done. . . . We go to a place where we will not suffer as we have suffered here, but where we will continue to grow, accumulating knowledge and developing and being useful under the plan of the Almighty made possible through the Atonement of the Son of God."

(Gordon B. Hinckley, *Ensign,* Oct. 1996, 73)

MARCH 10
Family Worship

Wednesday, 10 Mar. 1841: President Brigham Young of the Quorum of the Twelve, then on a mission in Great Britain, issues a letter for publication in the *Millennial Star*: "Heads of families should always take the charge of family worship, and call their family together at a seasonable hour, and not wait for every person to get through with all they may have to say or do. If it were my prerogative to adopt a plan for family prayer, it would be the following: Call your family or household together every morning and evening, previous to coming to the table, and bow before the Lord to offer up your thanksgiving for His mercies and providential care of you" (*HC* 4:309).

"Whether we are young or old, single or married, whether we have children at home or have become empty nesters, family home evening can increase unity and love in our homes. . . . You may not always feel like praying when you finally do get together, but it will pay great dividends if you persevere."

(James E. Faust, *Ensign,* Jun. 2003, 3–4)

MARCH 11
Scripture Study

Friday, 11 Mar. 1842: An elder of the Church, Francis Gladden Bishop, is brought before the Church High Council of Nauvoo, accused of "having received, written, and published or taught certain 'revelations' and doctrines not consistent with the Doctrine & Covenants of the Church" (*HC* 4:550). When he reads parts of these revelations, the brethren are kept "laughing, when not overcome by sorrow and shame" at "the extreme of folly, nonsense, absurdity, falsehood and bombastic egotism" of this doctrine. He is forthwith unanimously disfellowshipped by the Council (*HC* 4:550).

"When you hear people, who profess to be Latter-day Saints, running off on tangents, on foolish notions and one-horse, cranky ideas, things that are obviously opposed to reason and to good sense, opposed to principles of righteousness and to the word of the Lord that has been revealed to men, you should know at once that they have not studied the principles of the gospel, and do not know very much about the gospel."

(Joseph F. Smith, *Gospel Doctrine*, 114)

MARCH 12
Temperance

Saturday, 12 Mar. 1836: Joseph Smith learns that a man by the name of Clark has frozen to death in the vicinity under the influence of "ardent spirits." Heavy snow had fallen on the previous day, and the Prophet, in response to the news of the death, writes: "O my God, how long will this monster intemperance find its victims on earth, me thinks until the earth is swept with the wrath and indignation of God and Christ's Kingdom becomes universal. O come Lord Jesus and cut short thy work in righteousness" (*DJJS,* 140). Though "intemperance" here refers to imbibing alcohol, it may also mean anything done to excess.

"The Apostle Peter spoke of the process by which a person can be made a 'partaker of the divine nature' (2 Pet. 1:4). . . . [An] attribute described by Peter as being part of the divine nature is *temperance.* A priesthood holder is *temperate.* This means he is restrained in his emotions and verbal expressions. He does things in moderation and is not given to overindulgence. In a word, he has self-control."

(Ezra Taft Benson, *Ensign,* Nov. 1986, 45, 47)

MARCH 13
Endurance

Monday, 13 Mar. 1843: "I wrestled with William Wall, the most expert wrestler in Ramus, and threw him" (*HC* 5:302). So writes Joseph Smith concerning his victory over the champion from a town some 25 miles due east of Nauvoo, "the bully of Ramus" (*DJJS*, 352–353). It was the same William Wall who would attempt to deliver a verbal message on June 26, 1844, to Joseph Smith from his uncle, John Smith, the day after Joseph and Hyrum were imprisoned at Carthage Jail. On that occasion, the guard refused to allow Joseph and William to speak with each other (*HC* 6:590). When Joseph was murdered by a mob on the following day, this ended the lifelong mission of spiritually "wrestling with God" on behalf of the Saints.

"From the time these distant valleys began to be settled, until now, there has scarcely been a day but what I have felt [a] twenty-five ton weight, as it were, upon me, in exercising faith to keep this people from destroying themselves; but if any of them can exercise faith enough for themselves, and wish to excuse me, I will take my faith back."

(Brigham Young, *Journal of Discourses*, 1:166)

MARCH 14
Virtue

Tuesday, 14 Mar. 1843: Jedediah M. Grant inquires of Joseph Smith why the latter had turned pale and lost strength while blessing children at a meeting the previous evening. The Prophet's answer is instructive: "I saw that Lucifer would exert his influence to destroy the children that I was blessing, and I strove with all the faith and spirit that I had to seal upon them a blessing that would secure their lives upon the earth; and so much virtue went out of me into the children, that I became weak, from which I have not yet recovered." Referring to the case of the woman touching the garment of Jesus (Luke 8), he continues, "The virtue here referred to is the spirit of life; and a man who exercises great faith in administering to the sick, blessing little children, or confirming, is liable to become weakened" (*HC* 5:303). Whether nurturing or being nurtured, we look to the Lord as the source of all vitality.

"You cannot lift another soul until you are standing on higher ground than he is."

(Harold B. Lee, *Stand Ye in Holy Places,* 187)

MARCH 15

Preparation

Tuesday, 15 Mar. 1831: About this time, the Prophet Joseph Smith inquires of the Lord about obtaining lands to accommodate the influx of Saints from the East (see *HC* 1:166–167). In response, the Lord gives a revelation (Section 48) indicating that the Saints are to assemble "for the present time" in Ohio (v. 1), but to prepare for a coming announcement about the ultimate gathering place (later revealed as Jackson County, Missouri). The counsel of the Lord is relevant to any day: "It must needs be necessary that ye save all the money that ye can, and that ye obtain all that ye can in righteousness, that in time ye may be enabled to purchase land for an inheritance, even the city" (D&C 48:4). Prudent financial planning may increase the means to bless our families and fellowmen.

MARCH 16
Music

Thursday, 16 Mar. 1836: From the Prophet Joseph Smith's journal: "At evening met the quorum of Singers in the Chapel [Kirtland Temple]. They performed admirably considering the advantages they have had" (*DJJS*, 141). If we can read between the lines, we might conclude that this early chorus was not quite the equal of the Tabernacle Choir, but still performed to the glory of God. Concerning the quality of our musical offerings, the lesson seems to be that the Lord requires "the heart and a willing mind" (D&C 64:34), more than an unnatural level of polish from an uncooperative voice.

"At temple dedications I have seen more tears of joy elicited by music than by the spoken word. I have read accounts of angelic choirs joining in these hymns of praise, and I think I have experienced this on several occasions. . . . Sacred music has a unique capacity to communicate our feelings of love for the Lord."

(Dallin H. Oaks, *Ensign,* Nov. 1994, 10)

MARCH 17
Relief Society

Thursday, 17 Mar. 1842: The "Female Relief Society of Nauvoo" is founded under the direction of Joseph Smith. Emma Smith is elected president, with Elizabeth Ann Whitney and Sarah M. Cleveland as counselors. The organization had its beginnings in projects for sewing shirts for the men working on the Nauvoo Temple. The Prophet wrote of his assurance that "with the resources they will have at command, they will fly to the relief of the stranger; they will pour in oil and wine to the wounded heart of the distressed; they will dry up the tears of the orphan and make the widow's heart to rejoice" (*HC* 4:567). The Relief Society grew to around 1,300 members by the time the Prophet was martyred, and has since become the largest such organization in the world.

"There is no sister so isolated, and her sphere so narrow but what she can do a great deal towards establishing the kingdom of God upon the earth."

(Eliza R. Snow, quoted by Ezra Taft Benson, *Ensign,* Nov. 1988, 97)

MARCH 18
Devotion

Monday, 18 Mar. 1833: The organization of the First Presidency in this dispensation is completed (*HC* 1:334). The keys to direct the affairs of the kingdom "belong always unto the Presidency of the High Priesthood" (D&C 81:2). A year previous, Sidney Rigdon and Jesse Gause had been selected as counselors to Joseph Smith; however, when Jesse Gause did not stay with his calling, Frederick G. Williams was chosen to take his place and given glorious promises contingent on his being "faithful unto the end" (D&C 81:6). Neither Sidney nor Frederick remained faithful, and others were eventually called. Despite these setbacks in the early organization of the priesthood, the First Presidency continued to direct the Church in accordance with the will of the Lord in His kingdom that would "stand for ever" (Dan. 2:44).

"All of us at some time will be released by one process or another. It matters not where we serve in this great cause, but how we serve."

(Gordon B. Hinckley, *Ensign,* May 1997, 84)

MARCH 19
The Book of Mormon

Friday, 19 Mar. 1830: The *Wayne Sentinel* in Palmyra, New York, publishes an announcement that states: "We are requested to announce that the 'Book of Mormon' will be ready for sale in the course of a week" (*CHFT*, 66). At last, a divine work that had laid silent for centuries was to be made public. The initial press run of 5,000 is humble in comparison to the nearly 100 million copies published since then. This unique volume proves "to the world that the holy scriptures are true, and that God [calls men] to his holy work in this age and generation, as well as in generations of old; Thereby showing that he is the same God yesterday, today, and forever. Amen" (D&C 20:11–12).

"This gift was prepared by the hand of the Lord over a period of more than a thousand years, then hidden up by Him so that it would be preserved in its purity for our generation. . . . Can anyone doubt that this book was meant for us and that in it we find great power, great comfort, and great protection?"

(Ezra Taft Benson, *Ensign,* Jan. 1992, 2–7)

MARCH 20
Overcoming Adversity

Wednesday, 20 Mar. 1839: Joseph Smith writes his inspired letter from Liberty Jail in Missouri that would later serve as the basis for Sections 121, 122, and 123. The Prophet and several colleagues had been held there under conditions of extraordinary deprivation since 30 November 1838. In stark contrast to the squalid environment in which they were confined, Section 121 affords the most sublime language in holy writ concerning the effectual operation of the Priesthood of God. Section 122 is an inspiring call to transcend adversity. Section 123 is an impassioned plea for the Saints to fulfill their duty to God and to their suffering families by bringing to light the injustices being heaped upon them. These treasures of wisdom, born from the womb of adversity, are a lasting reminder that the blessings of God flow "after much tribulation" (D&C 58:4).

"The great lesson of Job is that, 'in all this Job sinned not, nor charged God foolishly' (Job 1:22). Too often when adversity strikes, we use it as a justification to commit sin and turn away from the teachings of Jesus Christ, the prophets who lead us, and our family and friends."

(Robert D. Hales, *Ensign,* Nov. 1981, 19)

MARCH 21
Sustaining Good Government

Thursday, 21 Mar. 1844: A council is held in the "assembly room" at Nauvoo to discuss "the propriety of petitioning Congress for the privilege of raising troops to protect the making of settlements in the uncivilized portions of our continent" (*HC* 6:270). Elder Willard Richards is appointed chairman of a committee to help Joseph Smith draw up a "Memorial to Congress" to outline the council's ideas to protect future pioneering settlements. In this action, as in so many others, the Prophet attempts to work through governmental processes for the protection of the rights of Saints and all citizens.

"I wish that I could impress this sentiment [from Abraham Lincoln] . . . upon the heart of every Latter-day Saint . . . 'Let reverence for the law be breathed by every American mother to the lisping babe that prattles on her lap; let it be taught in schools, in seminaries and colleges . . . let it be preached from the pulpit, proclaimed in legislative halls, and enforced in courts of justice.'"

(Heber J. Grant, *Teachings of Presidents of the Church: Heber J. Grant*, 160)

MARCH 22
Example

Tuesday, 22 Mar. 1842: The Prophet takes note of a favorable report from the pen of Abraham Jonas, who had recently spent three days visiting in Nauvoo. The report, which appeared in the Columbus, Ohio, *Advocate,* extols the industry, intelligence, temperance, and law-abiding character of the people, qualities the author finds to be at variance with slanderous gossip being circulated by the ill-informed. In Joseph Smith he expected to find an "ignorant and tyrannical upstart," but found instead "a sensible, intelligent, companionable and gentlemanly man. . . . He appears to be much respected by all the people about him, and has their entire confidence. He is a fine looking man about thirty-six years of age, and has an interesting family" (*HC* 4:566).

Saturday, 23 Mar. 1833: On this day at Kirtland, a Church council convenes to discuss buying land in Kirtland, "upon which the Saints might build a Stake of Zion" (*HC* 1:335). Some three hours after looking into purchase options, they decide to acquire Peter French's farm for $5,000. "The French farm was purchased on account of the facilities found there for making brick, which was essential to the building up of the city" (*HC* 1:336). On May 6, the Lord commands the Saints to "commence a work of laying out and preparing a beginning and foundation of the city of the stake of Zion, here in the land of Kirtland, beginning at my house" (D&C 94:1). The city is to be laid out using the proposed Kirtland Temple as the starting point. Thus, through small preparatory deeds, the way was prepared for the initiation of temple-building in this last dispensation.

"There is a price to pay for success, fulfillment, accomplishment, and joy. . . . Preparation, work, study, and service are required to achieve and find happiness. Disobedience and lack of preparation carry a terrible price tag."

(James E. Faust, *Ensign,* May 2003, 52)

MARCH 24
Charity

Thursday, 24 Mar. 1842: The Prophet Joseph Smith attends a meeting in which the organization of the Relief Society, formally inaugurated a week earlier on March 17, is completed. To the presidency of Emma Smith and her two counselors are added a treasurer (Elvira Cole) and a secretary (Eliza R. Snow). The Prophet writes of the recent deprivations suffered by these noble women: "In the midst of their persecution, when the bread has been torn from their helpless offspring by their cruel oppressors, they have always been ready to open their doors to the weary traveler, to divide their scant pittance with the hungry, and from their robbed and impoverished wardrobes, to divide with the more needy and destitute" (*HC* 4:568).

MARCH 25
Forgiveness

Sunday, 25 Mar. 1832: At this time the Prophet Joseph Smith and his family are staying at the home of John Johnson in Hiram, Ohio. This morning, Joseph delivers a sermon on forgiveness, baptizing three individuals that afternoon. The day before, a mob of some two dozen drunken men had dragged Joseph from the house, stripped him of his clothes, beat him brutally, and tarred and feathered him. All through the night friends and family had removed the skin-searing tar, taking up large areas of skin in the process. Young 11-month-old Joseph Murdock Smith, one of two adopted twins, already suffering with measles, contracted pneumonia from the exposure that night, and died a few days later. Some of the mobbers were present at the Prophet's sermon (see *HC* 1:261–65).

MARCH 26
Testimony

Friday, 26 Mar. 1830: The *Wayne Sentinel* advertises that the Book of Mormon "is now for sale, wholesale and retail, at the Palmyra Bookstore, by Howard and Grandin." The text of the advertisement is Moroni's title page for the Book of Mormon, which identifies this sacred volume as a witness for the divinity of Jesus Christ, and as evidence of the great things the Lord had done for His people in establishing His covenant with them and laying the foundation of hope for the future. At last, the fullness of the gospel emerges "out of the ground" in words of eternal salvation that would "whisper out of the dust" (Isa. 29:4).

"I received a witness that the Book of Mormon is the word of God, and that supernal event became my hour of conversion. . . . If your soul is searching for a more profound testimony of Jesus Christ and His restored kingdom, I suggest, in conjunction with studying the Book of Mormon, there are four steps you can take which will lead you to your hour of conversion. These four steps are (1) Desire, (2) Works, (3) Prayer, and (4) Trust in the Lord."

(Robert K. Dellenbach, *Ensign,* Nov. 1990, 23)

MARCH 27
Obedience

Sunday, 27 Mar. 1836: The Kirtland Temple is dedicated—the culmination of nearly three years of intense effort and united sacrifice on the part of the faithful Saints. The dedicatory prayer delivered by the Prophet Joseph Smith on that occasion had been given to him earlier by revelation (D&C 109). It petitions the Lord, among other things, to bestow His glory and truth upon all those associated with His house so that they might faithfully discharge their duties in a way pleasing to Him: "O Lord God Almighty, hear us in these our petitions, and answer us from heaven, thy holy habitation, where thou sittest enthroned, with glory, honor, power, majesty, might, dominion, truth, justice, judgment, mercy, and an infinity of fulness, from everlasting to everlasting" (v. 77). The first temple in this dispensation is placed in service with shouts of "Hosanna to God and the Lamb" (v. 79).

"I made this my rule: When the Lord commands, do it."

(Joseph Smith, *HC* 2:170)

MARCH 28
Duty

Saturday, 28 Mar. 1835: The Quorum of Twelve Apostles, newly called, meet in a planning and confessional session to prepare for their coming mission to the eastern states. They ask the Prophet Joseph Smith to seek a revelation from the Lord "that we may look upon it when we are separated, that our hearts may be comforted. Our worthiness has not inspired us to make this request, but our unworthiness" (*HC* 2:210). In response, that same day, the Lord reveals the first portion of D&C 107 (substantially through verse 58, the balance coming at other times). Section 107—along with Sections 20 and 121—can be regarded as the eternal constitution of the Priesthood of God. All 100 verses of this magnificent revelation are summarized in the oft-cited 99th verse.

"There is much to do. . . . You must now make yourselves worthy and available. If you do not, the work will go on without you. . . . If you do not do your duty, those whom you could have taught but did not will eventually have their opportunity to hear the gospel from someone else, but what of you?"

(William R. Bradford, *Ensign,* Nov. 1981, 51)

MARCH 29
Truth

Sunday, 29 Mar. 1835: The School of the Prophets closed the last week of March so that the Elders might have "an opportunity to go forth and proclaim the Gospel, preparatory to the endowment" (*HC* 2:218). At the invitation of a Campbellite preacher, Elder William E. McLellin has participated in a public debate on the divinity of the Book of Mormon. Today Joseph Smith joins Elder McLellin for the third and final day of the debate, preaching to a congregation for three hours. Two listeners, touched by the truth, are baptized, followed by four more the next day.

"Those early disciples declared to those seeking truth, in plainness, that as the Holy Ghost rested upon them, filling their hearts with joy, they would know of the doctrine for themselves, whether it be of God or man. The Spirit of truth leads men to righteousness, but we must have a desire to seek truth and to take the time to form spiritual habits and respond to spiritual impressions if we are to keep our souls alive—and is not now the time to begin?"

(David B. Haight, *Ensign,* May 1988, 21)

MARCH 30
Diligence

⸎

Wednesday, 30 Mar. 1836: A remarkable meeting takes place in the Kirtland Temple attended by some 300 priesthood leaders. It lasts from 8:00 A.M. that day until 5:00 A.M. the next morning—21 hours in all (*HC* 2:430–433). Activities include special instructions from the Prophet Joseph Smith, the washing of the feet of the Twelve by the First Presidency, administration of the sacrament, review of priesthood duties and operations, a challenge to go forth in devoted service, and many marvelous spiritual manifestations for those brethren who remain throughout the night. The Prophet observes, "So shall this day be numbered and celebrated as a year of jubilee and time of rejoicing to the Saints of the Most High God." It should be noted that the spiritual character of this meeting, and not necessarily its length, should most be emulated!

"Hunger makes food very delicious. Hunger for the Gospel of Jesus Christ makes us enjoy [our] conferences."

(Heber J. Grant, *Teachings of Presidents of the Church: Heber J. Grant*, 7)

MARCH 31
Sociability

Friday, 31 Mar. 1834: The Prophet Joseph Smith goes on a date with his wife Emma. "Spent the afternoon at Mr. Lucian Woodworth's in company with Brother Hyrum, Heber C. Kimball, Orson Hyde, Wilford Woodruff, and Brother Chase, with our wives; had a good time, and feasted on a fat turkey" (*HC* 5:317). If we had been a "fly on the wall" on this occasion, we would no doubt have seen the Prophet in a display of his native good nature and charming sociability.

"One of the main problems in society today is that we spend less and less time together. Some, even when they are together, spend an extraordinary amount of time in front of the television, which robs them of personal time for reinforcing feelings of self-worth. . . . Time together is precious—time needed to encourage and to show how to do things. Less time together can result in loneliness, which may produce feelings of being unsupported, untreasured, and inadequate."

(James E. Faust, *Ensign,* June 2003, 5)

APRIL

It is required . . . of every steward, to render an account of his stewardship, both in time and in eternity.

—D&C 72:3

APRIL 1

Forgiveness

Friday, 1 Apr. 1836: A story about forgiveness unfolds this day concerning Leman Copley, a convert to the Church in March 1831 at age 50. Nevertheless, in 1834 he testified against Joseph's case in a trial brought by the Prophet against "Doctor" Philastus Hurlburt, who had made threats on Joseph's life. On this day, Copley comes to Joseph in Kirtland seeking forgiveness for his false testimony. Even *this* show of contrition will be short-lived, since Copley will later join one apostate group after another. But the real lesson in this story is Joseph's reaction to the plea for forgiveness from a detractor who had been the source of significant harm and had openly impugned the Prophet's character. He "readily" forgives him and accepts him back into the Church by baptism according to his desire (see *HC* 2:433).

APRIL 2
The Nature of God

Sunday, 2 Apr. 1843: On this day, at a morning Church meeting in Ramus, the Prophet listens to Orson Hyde preach a sermon in which he says, "It is our privilege to have the Father and Son dwelling in our hearts" (*HC* 5:323). Afterwards, during a luncheon at the home of the Prophet's sister, Sophronia McCleary, the Prophet tells Elder Hyde that he is going to offer some corrections to his sermon. Orson Hyde replies, "They shall be thankfully received." The Prophet then shares with him the important insights included in Section 130 among others: "John 14:23—The appearing of the Father and the Son, in that verse, is a personal appearance; and the idea that the Father and the Son dwell in a man's heart is an old sectarian notion, and is false" (v. 3).

APRIL 3
Keys of the Priesthood

Sunday, 3 Apr. 1836: Today is "one of the most eventful days in the history of the Church," according to President Joseph Fielding Smith (*CHMR,* 2:78). A week earlier the Kirtland Temple had been dedicated with an outpouring of many heavenly manifestations. After the administration of the sacrament, Joseph and Oliver Cowdery pray in seclusion and then receive the visions recorded in Section 110, wherein the Savior, Moses, Elias (the angel Gabriel, who is Noah; see *Doctrine & Covenants Student Manual,* 275–276), and Elijah visit in succession, each of the latter three committing keys to the First and Second Elders of the Church.

APRIL 4

Persistence

Tuesday, 4 Apr. 1843: "Spent five hours preaching to Esquire Backman, Chancery Robinson, and Backenstos. Backman said, 'Almost thou persuadest me to be a Christian'" (*HC* 5:326). This is Joseph Smith's diary entry about a trip to Carthage, Illinois, where he was addressing another legal issue in the endless stream against the Church and its Saints. Mr. Backman was a lawyer whose services the Prophet used on occasion. Mr. Robinson was a local citizen, and Jacob Backenstos was a supporter of the cause of the Church. The Prophet invested many hours in doing missionary work at a time of pressing concerns. Are we so distracted by other things that we do not take the time to spread the good news?

"My understanding is that the most important mission that I have in this life is: first, to keep the commandments of God, as they have been taught to me; and next, to teach them to my Father's children who do not understand them."

(George Albert Smith, *The Teachings of George Albert Smith*, 149)

APRIL 5

Teamwork

Sunday, 5 Apr. 1829: The Prophet Joseph mentions Oliver Cowdery for the first time (see *HC* 1:32). To avoid persecution and to complete the translation of the Book of Mormon, Joseph had moved to Harmony, Pennsylvania, where he and Emma lived near her parents' farm. Because of the responsibility to care for his family and earn a living, the Prophet felt the weight of heavy burdens, and the Lord had told him in March to "Stop, and stand still until I command thee, and I will provide means whereby thou mayest accomplish the thing which I have commanded thee" (D&C 5:34). In direct fulfillment of this promise, 22-year-old Oliver arrives and will soon assist Joseph as a scribe in completing the translation from the ancient record. In just three short months, beginning on the 7th of April, they will finish their task.

APRIL 6

The Restored Church

Tuesday, 6 Apr. 1830: The Church is formally organized in accordance with instructions given by revelation, which teaches that this is the Lord's birthday (D&C 20:1). More than fifty persons are present at the Whitmer log home in Fayette, New York, to participate in the event, including the six who function as incorporators to meet state requirements: Joseph Smith, Hyrum Smith, Oliver Cowdery, Peter Whitmer, Jr., Samuel H. Smith (the Prophet's younger brother), and David Whitmer. The agenda is simple: a vote by the participants sustaining the action and the leadership, Joseph Smith ordaining Oliver Cowdery an elder of the Church (and vice versa), administration of the sacrament, confirmation of members and bestowal of the gift of the Holy Ghost, and miscellaneous ordinations. Section 21 is received, reiterating that Joseph serves as the Lord's mouthpiece to the newborn Church (see *HC* 1:74–79).

APRIL 7
The Nature of God and Man

Sunday, 7 Apr. 1844: The 14th annual General Conference of the Church had convened two days previous to this in Nauvoo. Apostates and others are determined to disrupt the services and expect Joseph Smith to focus on them. But instead, on April 7th, the third day of the conference, Joseph Smith avoids confrontation by delivering what many people consider his most inspired and eloquent sermon—the King Follett discourse—in honor of the passing of one of the esteemed local members of the Church the previous month (see also March 9). Before a congregation of some 20,000 Saints, the Prophet unfolds astounding insights into the character of God, the premortal existence, immortal intelligence, the relationship of man to God, forgiveness of sins, the second death, and much more (see *HC* 6:302–318).

"I would that all men and women upon the earth were able to grasp the significance of the experiences of earth-life and would thereby gain 'a nobler estimate of man,' that as God is, man may become."

(Harold B. Lee, *The Teachings of Harold B. Lee,* 160)

APRIL 8

First Principles

Saturday, 8 Apr. 1843: Contention had arisen among certain Saints concerning the meaning of the four beasts mentioned in Revelation 5:8. One brother had even been called before the High Council for his views on the subject. Joseph chides all factions with good humor and, with some reluctance, goes on to explain the symbolism (see Section 77). He points the Saints to logic, the scriptures, and revelation for such knowledge. "I refer to the prophets to qualify my observations which I make, so that the young elders who know so much, may not rise up like a flock of hornets and sting me" (*HC* 5:341). He emphatically states, "Declare the first principles, and let mysteries alone, lest ye be overthrown" (*HC* 5:344).

"Teach and live the first principles of the gospel, and let the mysteries of heaven wait until you get to heaven."

(Heber J. Grant, *Teachings of Presidents of the Church: Heber J. Grant*, 3)

APRIL 9

Personal Revelation

Thursday, 9 Apr. 1829: Around this time, several revelations are given concerning Oliver Cowdery's assistance in bringing forth the Book of Mormon (Sections 6, 8, and 9; see *HC* 1:32–38). When Oliver seeks a witness, the Lord responds, "Yea, behold, I will tell you in your mind and in your heart, by the Holy Ghost, which shall come upon you and which shall dwell in your heart. Now, behold, this is the spirit of revelation. . . . Remember that without faith you can do nothing; therefore ask in faith" (D&C 8:2–3, 10). When Oliver exhibits fear and fails to secure the gift, the Lord instructs him further: "Behold, you have not understood; you have supposed that I would give it unto you, when you took no thought save it was to ask me. But, behold, I say unto you, that you must study it out in your mind; then you must ask me if it be right, and if it is right I will cause that your bosom shall burn within you; therefore, you shall feel that it is right. But if it be not right you shall have no such feelings, but you shall have a stupor of thought that shall cause you to forget the thing which is wrong . . ." (D&C 9:7–9).

APRIL 10
Purity

Sunday, 10 Apr. 1842: The Prophet Joseph preaches a spirited and candid sermon on repentance in the grove west of the Nauvoo Temple. Some choice comments are captured in the journal of Wilford Woodruff: "If you wish to go where God is, you must be like God, or possess the principles which God possesses, for if we are not drawing towards God in principle, we are going from Him and drawing towards the devil. . . . Search your hearts, and see if you are like God. I have searched mine, and feel to repent of all my sins. . . . While our hearts are filled with evil, and we are studying evil, there is no room in our hearts for good, or studying good. . . . Add to your faith virtue, to virtue knowledge, and seek for every good thing. The Church must be cleansed, and I proclaim against all iniquity" (*HC* 4:588).

APRIL 11

Testimony Bearing

Sunday, 11 Apr. 1830: Just five days after the organization of the Church in Fayette, New York, Oliver Cowdery, preaches "the first public discourse that was delivered by any of our number" (*HC* 1:81). It is fitting that "the second elder of this church" (D&C 20:3) thus literally becomes "the first preacher of this church unto the church, and before the world" (D&C 21:12). Several people come forward and submit to the ordinance of baptism in Seneca Lake. One of those whom Oliver baptizes is 15-year-old Elizabeth Ann Whitmer. She and Oliver marry in Jackson County, Missouri, on December 18, 1832 (see *HC* 1:32).

"The Lord gave others to stand with Joseph to verify what the Lord had done. They were with the Prophet when the heavens were opened. Oliver Cowdery preached the first missionary sermon the first Sunday after the Church was organized. He went into the mission field to proclaim what he knew by what he saw and heard and felt."

(Henry B. Eyring, *Ensign,* Nov. 2003, 89)

APRIL 12
Missionary Work

Wednesday, 12 Apr. 1843: The steamer *Amaranth*—the first up the Mississippi River this season—arrives in Nauvoo around noon, while a special three-day conference of the priesthood (including most of the Twelve) is being conducted. The ship delivered some 240 immigrant convert Saints from England, under the leadership of Lorenzo Snow. The Prophet Joseph Smith greets them in person with great joy. A few hours later, at 5:00 P.M., the *Maid of Iowa* arrives with about 200 more Saints from England, under the leadership of Levi Richards and Parley P. Pratt. The Prophet notes: "I was rejoiced to meet them in such good health and fine spirits; for they were equal to any that had ever come to Nauvoo" (*HC* 5:354).

APRIL 13
Revelation for the Church

Saturday, 13 Apr. 1833: On this day, Jared Carter comes to Joseph Smith to present him with a letter from one of his brothers, asking the Prophet to respond to some of his questions. Joseph's answers have become much-quoted words of eternal truth for our benefit today. For example, "it is contrary to the economy of God for any member of the Church, or any one, to receive instructions for those in authority, higher than themselves; therefore you will see the inpropriety [sic] of giving heed to them" (*HC* 1:338).

"The father and mother of the family are entitled to revelation for the ruling of their family and all of their interests. The bishop is entitled to the revelations of God for his flock; the stake president for the stake, and the President of the Church, of course, is the only one that holds the keys actively and totally, and he will receive the revelations for the Church. . . . God is not the author of confusion."

(Spencer W. Kimball, *Teachings of Spencer W. Kimball*, 453)

APRIL 14
The Book of Mormon

Saturday, 14 Apr. 1832: Brigham Young is baptized after two years of intensive study and prayer centered on a Book of Mormon his brother Phineas had given him. Phineas purchased the copy from the Prophet's younger brother, Samuel Harrison Smith. Samuel also provided a copy to Reverend John P. Greene, husband of Phineas's sister, Rhoda. Both were subsequently converted. Brigham Young had given his copy of the Book of Mormon to his sister, Fanny Young Murray, the mother-in-law of Heber C. Kimball, who, along with his family, also became converted because of it. Young Samuel had returned home somewhat discouraged from this early mission to upstate New York—unaware at the time that his labors would eventually yield such extraordinary fruit (see *CHFT*, 74–75).

APRIL 15

Service

Tuesday, 15 Apr. 1834: "Hauled a load of hay; and on Wednesday plowed and sowed oats for Brother Frederick G. Williams" (*HC* 2:50). That's all Joseph Smith wrote as a journal entry for an entire two-day period, but it reveals a glimpse into the magnanimous character of Joseph Smith the Prophet. The Prophet Joseph not only understood that he shouldn't live off the labors of the people, but here he is, hitching the plow to the horse, furrowing the ground row after row, and laying in seed so his aging counselor will have a crop in Kirtland this fall. A short time previous, Joseph gave his own horse to President Williams out of the goodness of his generous heart. Acts like these are pervasive throughout Joseph's entire life. It is the *small* things that reveal great character, and Joseph's was great.

"During the first 30 years of His life in Nazareth, Jesus apparently drew little attention to Himself even though He was living a sinless life (see Matt. 13:54–56; Mark 6:2–3). That should encourage us to do better in our own quiet and humble way without drawing attention to ourselves."

(William W. Parmley, *Ensign,* Nov. 2003, 94)

APRIL 16

Resurrection

Sunday, 16 Apr. 1843: The Prophet Joseph Smith speaks at the temple in Nauvoo for about two hours on the death of Lorenzo D. Barnes, the first missionary to die while serving on foreign soil. Joseph stated: "Those who have died in Jesus Christ may expect to enter into all that fruition of joy when they come forth, which they possessed or anticipated here. . . . All your losses will be made up to you in the resurrection, provided you continue faithful. . . . The expectation of seeing my friends in the morning of the resurrection cheers my soul and makes me bear up against the evils of life. It is like their taking a long journey, and on their return we meet them with increased joy" (*HC* 5:361–362).

APRIL 17

Fathers

Tuesday, 17 Apr. 1838: On January 12, Joseph Smith and Sidney Rigdon were forced to flee Kirtland on horseback, closely pursued by a bloodthirsty mob. In Missouri, Brigham Young seeks counsel from the Prophet, who receives for him this direction from the Lord on April 17th: "Verily, thus saith the Lord, let my servant Brigham Young go unto the place which he has bought . . . and there provide for his family until an effectual door is opened for the support of his family, until I shall command him to go hence, and not to leave his family until they are amply provided for" (*HC* 3:23).

"Yours is the basic and inescapable responsibility to stand as head of the family. . . . It carries with it a mandate that fathers provide for the needs of their families. Those needs are more than food, clothing, and shelter. Those needs include righteous direction and the teaching, by example as well as precept, of basic principles of honesty, integrity, service, respect for the rights of others, and an understanding that we are accountable for that which we do in this life, not only to one another but also the God of heaven, who is our Eternal Father."

(Gordon B. Hinckley, *Ensign,* Nov. 1993, 60)

APRIL 18
Listen to the Spirit

Friday, 18 Apr. 1834: The Prophet Joseph Smith, accompanied by Sidney Rigdon, Oliver Cowdery, and Zebedee Coltrin, leave Kirtland to attend a conference of the Church elsewhere in the state. "After dark, we were hailed by a man who desired to ride. We were checked by the Spirit, and refused. He professed to be sick, but in a few minutes was joined by two others, who followed us hard, cursing and swearing; but we were successful in escaping their hands, through the providence of the Lord" (*HC* 2:50). "Checked by the Spirit, and refused"—six short words of wisdom indispensable to all discerning and responsive sons and daughters of God.

"I would have been in the spirit world a great many years ago, if I had not followed the promptings of the still small voice. . . . I have been blessed at times with certain gifts and graces, certain revelations and ministrations; but with them all I have never found anything that I could place more dependence upon than the still small voice of the Holy Ghost."

(Wilford Woodruff, *Journal of Discourses*, 21:195–196)

APRIL 19

Prayer

Tuesday, 19 Apr. 1834: Joseph Smith, Sidney Rigdon, Oliver Cowdery, and Zebedee Coltrin arrive in Norton (a branch outside of Kirtland) to conduct a two-day conference, which is to begin the next day. After arrangements are made for temporary quarters at the home of Jonathan Taylor, the Prophet recalls in his journal: "We soon retired to the wilderness, where we united in prayer and supplication for the blessings of the Lord to be given unto His Church. . . . and that I might have strength, and wisdom, and understanding sufficient to lead the people of the Lord . . . that they may be no more cast down forever" (*HC* 2:50–51). The image of the Prophet and his colleagues gathered "in the wilderness" in united prayer for strength in their callings is a reminder to step aside from our duties frequently and invoke the blessings of the Lord.

APRIL 20
Give Your All

~~~

Saturday, 20 Apr. 1839: "The last of the Saints left Far West" (*HC* 3:326). This represents the closing of the Missouri chapter wherein the Saints were prevented by their enemies from carrying out the Lord's commandment to build a community and temple at Far West: "And in one year from this day [April 26, 1838] let them re-commence laying the foundation of my house" (D&C 115:11). But it was not to be; instead, the Lord allowed the Saints to build the Nauvoo Temple.

"In the final letter recorded in the Book of Mormon from Mormon to his son Moroni, he gave counsel that applies to our day. . . . 'And now, my beloved son, notwithstanding their hardness, let us labor diligently . . . for we have a labor to perform whilst in this tabernacle of clay, that we may conquer the enemy of all righteousness . . .' (Moro. 9:6). You and I have a similar labor to perform now—to conquer the enemy and rest our souls in the kingdom."

(Ezra Taft Benson, *Ensign,* Nov. 1987, 85)

APRIL 21
Humility

Sunday, 21 Apr. 1834: Joseph Smith writes a letter of admonition from Kirtland to the brethren in Zion (Missouri) replying to their correspondence. He writes: "we now commence [to answer your letters], after giving thanks to our Heavenly Father for every expression of His goodness in preserving our unprofitable lives to the present time, and for the health and other blessings which we now enjoy through His mercies" (*HC* 1:340). Here we see the gratitude and touching humility of this great Prophet of the Restoration who "has done more, save Jesus only, for the salvation of men in this world, than any other man that ever lived in it" (D&C 135:3); and yet he considers himself an unprofitable servant.

"When our successes are received without proper acknowledgment to Him who is the grantor of all blessings, these same successes often lead to false pride and a deterioration of the virtues that bring us to faith. . . . Whatever our station in life, whatever our achievements, no matter how great, a submissive heart and a humble spirit are still fundamental to our faith."

(Richard C. Edgley, *Ensign,* May 1993, 11)

APRIL 22

Adversity

Monday, 22 Apr. 1839: The Prophet composes a moving memorial of the Saints' cruel persecution at the hands of the Missouri mobs, at the same time giving thanks for the Lord's steadying hand and calling for civil redress. "The conduct of the Saints, under their accumulated wrongs and sufferings, has been praiseworthy. . . . All conspire to raise them in the estimation of all good and virtuous men, and has secured them the favor and approbation of Jehovah, and a name as imperishable as eternity. . . . Marvel not, then, if you are persecuted. . . . Afflictions, persecutions, imprisonments, and death, we must expect, according to the scriptures" (*HC* 3:329–331). He also quotes this verse: "Short though bitter was their pain, Everlasting is their joy" (*HC* 3:330).

APRIL 23

Stewardship

Wednesday, 23 Apr. 1834: During a council meeting with other Church leaders, Joseph the Prophet receives Section 104 concerning the temporal welfare of the Church and the pattern for the Saints regarding the poor and needy (*HC* 2:54–60). In an earlier revelation, the Lord had declared, "And it pleaseth God that he hath given all these things unto man; for unto this end were they made to be used, with judgment, not to excess, neither by extortion" (D&C 59:20). The word "extortion" seems to imply situations where individuals misuse the abundance of the Lord's earth for their own selfish purposes without concern for the needs of others— especially the poor and needy.

"A major reason why there is famine in some parts of the world is because evil men have used the vehicle of goverment to abridge the freedom that men need to produce abundantly."

(Ezra Taft Benson, *Doctrine and Covenants Student Manual*, 254).

APRIL 24
Family Recreation

Monday, 24 Apr. 1843: "In the morning I took my children [on] a pleasure ride in the carriage" (*HC* 5:369). The Prophet Joseph Smith thus reminds us again of the need to balance professional duties, personal affairs, and Church service with attention to the needs of the family. Perhaps the Prophet used his humor on this occasion to amuse his children in good sport, but also never lost an opportunity to teach them in memorable ways how the gospel leads to eternal and lasting joy. As John said, "I have no greater joy than to hear that my children walk in truth" (3 John 1:4).

"I trust that all Latter-day Saints' homes will be such that our children can obtain wholesome pleasures without seeking them outside. I pray my heavenly Father that he will instill in the hearts of the mothers and fathers of Israel a desire to look more carefully after their children."

(Reed Smoot, CR, Oct. 1916, 40)

APRIL 25

Persecution

Thursday, 25 Apr. 1833: The Prophet writes in his journal: "In the month of April [1833], the first regular mob rushed together, in Independence, to consult upon a plan, for the removal, or immediate destruction, of the Church in Jackson county. The number of the mob was about three hundred. A few of the first Elders met in secret, and prayed to Him who said to the wind, 'Be still,' to frustrate them in their wicked designs. The mob . . . became a little the worse for liquor and broke up in a regular Missouri 'row,' showing a determined resolution that every man would 'carry his own head'" (*HC* 1:342). The Saints were driven from Jackson County later that year. For the Saints of the living God, the pathway to peace and eternal joy has always led through the valley of persecution in every age.

APRIL 26
Fulfilment

Friday, 26 Apr. 1839: A few minutes after midnight, a number of the Twelve Apostles gather with a few Saints at the temple site in Far West, Missouri, for an unusual meeting. These brethren ordain Wilford Woodruff and George A. Smith Apostles and then two others as Seventies. After prayers and a hymn ("Adam-ondi-Ahman"), the Twelve take leave of those assembled and depart into the night. Why this clandestine midnight meeting? The angry mobs that had driven the Saints away the previous fall swore that no such meeting would take place. They were aware of a revelation given on July 8, 1838, announcing that the Twelve would "take leave of my saints in the city of Far West, on the twenty-sixth day of April next, on the building-spot of my house, saith the Lord" (D&C 118:5) to perform missionary duties in Europe. The mobs planned to prove "Joe Smith" a false prophet by preventing such a gathering on that date. Imagine their shock when they learned later the same day that the event had already occurred just as the Lord had commanded.

APRIL 27
Miracles from Faith

Tuesday, 27 Apr. 1830: What Joseph Smith characterized as "the first miracle . . . done in the Church" (*HC* 1:83) provides dramatic evidence for the operation of the Spirit in the new Church. During one of several meetings held in Colesville, New York, the Prophet urges one of the Knight sons to pray regarding the truthfulness of the gospel. The following morning Newel enters the woods to pray, but finds he cannot speak. Alarmed at his troubled appearance, his wife calls for Joseph to come. The Prophet finds his friend displaying bizarre behavior, being "caught up off the floor of the apartment and tossed about most fearfully" (*HC* 1:82). Joseph catches Newel by the hand and, on the basis of Newel's faith, rebukes the evil spirit in him through the power of God. Newel observes the devil leaving him, and the scene is replaced by a manifestation of "the visions of eternity" through the Spirit. Most of those who witnessed this miracle joined the Church.

APRIL 28
Women of Charity

Thursday, 28 Apr. 1842: Joseph Smith meets in the afternoon with members of the "Female Relief Society" (*HC* 4:602), which had been formally organized on March 17. The Prophet's remarks center on 1 Corinthians 12 and the blessing of spiritual gifts. He also said: "This is a charitable Society, and according to your natures; it is natural for females to have feelings of charity and benevolence. You are now placed in a situation in which you can act according to those sympathies which God has planted in your bosoms. . . . If you live up to your privileges, the angels cannot be restrained from being your associates" (*HC* 4:605).

"I have seen examples in every branch, ward, and stake I have visited, and I have heard of the goodness of the women of this Church in letters that bear testimony that 'Charity Never Faileth.' . . . Your efforts to assist and help others have become so much a part of your personal style that, for the most part, they are spontaneous, instinctive, immediate."

(Elaine L. Jack, *Ensign,* Nov. 1996, 91)

APRIL 29

Commitment

Wednesday, 29 Apr. 1840: Wilford Woodruff pens a letter to the publishers of the *Times & Seasons* describing his missionary labors to that point in England. "Traveled 4,469 miles. Held 230 meetings. Established preaching 53 places. Planted 47 churches which included 1,500 Saints, 28 elders, 110 priests, 24 teachers, 10 deacons. Attended conferences 14. Baptized 336 persons, which included 57 preachers, 2 clerks of the Church of England. Assisted in the baptism 86 others. Confirmed 420. Assisted in confirmation 50 others. Ordained 18 elders, 97 priests, 34 teachers, 1 deacon. Blessed 120 children. Administered unto 120 sick persons. Assisted in procuring 1,000 pounds sterling for printing *Millennial Star*, three thousand copies of the Latter-day Saints hymns, and five thousand copies of the Book of Mormon. Assisted in emigrating 200 Saints to America. Wrote 200 letters. Received 112 letters. Mobs came against me 4 [times]" (*CHFT*, 230). This gives us an inkling of the true meaning of the word "commitment."

APRIL 30
Obligation

Monday, 30 Apr. 1832: Section 83 is received by the Prophet Joseph Smith as he sits in council with the priesthood in Independence, Missouri, endeavoring to organize the Church, so it would be independent of every incumbrance beneath the celestial kingdom by . . . covenants of mutual friendship and . . . love" (*HC* 1:269). The Lord makes clear that women and children have claim upon their husbands for their support and maintenance, and that the Church has an obligation to provide for the needs of widows, orphans, and the poor: "And the storehouse shall be kept . . . and widows and orphans shall be provided for, as also the poor" (D&C 83:6).

"We shall go on in this work. There will always be a need. Hunger and want and catastrophes will ever be with us. And there will always be those whose hearts have been touched by the light of the gospel who will be willing to serve and work and lift the needy of the earth."

(Gordon B. Hinckley, *Ensign,* May 2004, 61)

MAY

Thy faithfulness is stronger than the cords of death.

—D&C 121:44

MAY 1
Wealth As a Stumbling Block

Monday, 1 May 1842: Wealth has always been a stumbling block for man in separating him from God. Worldly treasures become a substitute for God when allowed to become a focal point. Conversely, God seems to make allowances for, and provide special spiritual blessings to, the poor. During a sermon at the "grove" near the Nauvoo Temple this day, Joseph Smith remarks: "The rich can only get them in the temple, the poor may get them on the mountain top as did Moses. The rich cannot be saved without charity, giving to feed the poor when and how God requires, as well as building" (*HC* 4:608). In the future, as head of the Church, President Young will voice his concern that the Saints in latter times (meaning our day) will be tested much more by their wealth than the Saints ever were by their poverty.

"Generally speaking, it was the poor who heard the message, the poor were gathered in, and the poor have accomplished what we see."

(Charles W. Nibley, *Improvement Era*, 33:662)

MAY 2

Consecration

Monday, 2 May 1842: An editorial appears in the *Times & Seasons* concerning the temple construction: "This noble edifice is progressing with great rapidity. . . . While the busy multitudes have thus been engaged in their several vocations . . . and working one-tenth of their time, others have not been less forward in bringing their tithings and consecrations for the same great object. Never since the foundation of this Church was laid, have we seen manifested a greater willingness to comply with the requisitions of Jehovah, a more ardent desire to do the will of God, more strenuous exertions used, or greater sacrifices made than there have been since the Lord said, 'Let the Temple be built by the tithing of my people'" (*HC* 4:608–609).

"We tend to think of consecration only as yielding up, when divinely directed, our material possessions. But ultimate consecration is the yielding up of oneself to God. *Heart, soul,* and *mind* were the encompassing words of Christ in describing the first commandment, which is constantly, not periodically, operative (see Matt. 22:37)."

(Neal A. Maxwell, *Ensign,* May 2002, 36)

MAY 3
The Name of Christ's Church

Saturday, 3 May 1834: In a journal entry, the Prophet Joseph Smith includes material from a recent conference of "the Elders of the Church of Christ" at Kirtland in which "The Church of the Latter-Day Saints" is adopted as the name of the Church (see *HC* 2:62). Previous names included "The Church of Christ," "The Church of Jesus Christ," "Church of God," etc. However, four years later, on April 26, 1838, the Lord settled the issue: "For thus shall my church be called in the last days, even The Church of Jesus Christ of Latter-day Saints" (D&C 115:4). With this, all previous variations of the name of the Church were set aside. It is the Lord's Church. He is at its head.

"The First Presidency has repeatedly requested that we not refer to ourselves as 'The Mormon Church' but by the name the Lord gave His Church by revelation: 'The Church of Jesus Christ of Latter-day Saints' (D&C 115:4)."

(Dallin H. Oaks, *With Full Purpose of Heart*, 72)

MAY 4
Endowment of Truth

Wednesday, 4 May 1842: At a meeting in the upper story of the Prophet's redbrick store in Nauvoo, Joseph Smith introduces the sacred temple endowment for the first time in this dispensation. "There was nothing made known to these men but what will be made known to all the Saints of the last days, so soon as they are prepared to receive, and a proper place is prepared to communicate them, even to the weakest of the Saints; therefore let the Saints be diligent in building the Temple" (*HC* 5:2).

"President Brigham Young made this observation about the endowment: 'Your *endowment* is, to receive all those ordinances in the House of the Lord, which are necessary for you, after you have departed this life, to enable you to walk back to the presence of the Father, passing the angels who stand as sentinels . . . and gain your eternal exaltation in spite of earth and hell.' . . . Our understanding of the significance of the endowment expands as we regularly participate in the holy ordinances in behalf of those deceased."

(David B. Haight, *Ensign,* May 1992, 15–16)

MAY 5

Edification

Saturday, 5 May 1831: The Prophet Joseph Smith receives Section 50 about this time (the record shows May of 1831, but the precise day is not given). It was given because Parley P. Pratt and several others were concerned about unusual behavior and manifestations they had observed among some of the people in the area. The Lord makes it clear that only that which edifies and comes through the Spirit of truth is of God. The word "edify" itself is related to a Latin root meaning to build a temple—hence the meaning to "build up" a person morally and spiritually. (*HC* 1:173).

"How do we recognize the promptings of the Spirit? That which is of Christ does edify, and if we have that feeling of edification, then we may know that the Holy Spirit, the Holy Ghost, is speaking to us. If we are in an attitude of prayer, if we are in an attitude of anxiously seeking the direction of the Spirit, we will receive it."

(Gordon B. Hinckley, *Ensign,* Aug. 2000, 2)

MAY 6
Grace for Grace

Monday, 6 May 1833: Section 93 is received, blessing the Saints with extraordinary new spiritual truths as well as exhortations to "bring up your children in light and truth" (v. 40). Some celebrated passages from this section are: "And truth is knowledge of things as they are, and as they were, and as they are to come" (v. 24); "The glory of God is intelligence, or, in other words, light and truth" (v. 36). On the same day, Section 94 was also given, with directions for erecting certain buildings in Kirtland (see *HC* 1:346–347). However, these buildings were never completed, since the erection of the temple in Kirtland took obvious precedence and consumed all of the energy and resources of the Saints before they were forced to flee because of persecution.

MAY 7
Organize Yourselves

Wednesday, 7 May 1834: The Prophet Joseph Smith, as commander in chief of Zion's Camp, takes time to organize his men at New Portage (about 50 miles away from Kirtland) before they continue their 1000-mile march. The Prophet imparts an effective leadership structure to the group of some 130 men (most of them very young) and 20 baggage wagons. Some of the Prophet's organizing principles included careful resource management; leadership based on delegation, accountability, and the voice of the people; an internal team structure, with specific duties for everyone; and a wise balance of the tem-poral and the spiritual (see *HC* 2:64–65).

"Remember this as a guideline in whatever position you are called to serve: 'What e'er thou art, act well thy part.'"
(David O. McKay, CR, Apr. 1969, 95)

MAY 8
Prophecy and Revelation

Tuesday, 8 May 1838: Joseph Smith writes for the *Elders' Journal* to answer the questions most frequently put to him by people outside the Church (*HC* 3:28–30). Among his answers is a beautiful reiteration of the latter-day witness of Christ. Here is a sampling: Question: "Is there anything in the Bible which licenses you to believe in revelation now-a-days?" Answer: "Is there anything that does not authorize us to believe so? If there is, we have, as yet, not been able to find it." We see that the Prophet accords to prophecy and revelation a universal legitimacy as the Lord's means, through the Holy Spirit, of bestowing spiritual gifts for the ongoing blessing of all His children.

"Of the sacred gifts of the Spirit, one that I believe has impact on each of our lives is the gift of prophecy or revelation. This gift is different from the priesthood office of prophet. The gift of prophecy is the testimony of Jesus. . . . Every Church member, if faithful, has the right to receive revelation for his or her personal blessing."

(Robert D. Hales, *Ensign,* Feb. 2002, 15)

MAY 9
Stand in Holy Places

~~~

Thursday, 9 May 1839: Joseph, Emma, and their children leave Quincy, Illinois, on their way to the future site of Nauvoo. The Saints had been driven from Missouri with Governor Boggs' infamous extermination order at their heels. On April 25th, Joseph and other Church leaders scoped out land near Commerce, Illinois, where it was hoped the Saints could settle unmolested from their enemies. On May 1, Joseph and a "relief committee" purchased a 135-acre farm from Hugh White for $5,000 and a farm from Dr. Isaac Galland for $9,000 for the gathering of the Saints (*HC* 3:342). Joseph records: "Took up my residence in a small log house on the bank of the river, about one mile south of Commerce City, hoping that I and my friends may here find a resting place for a little season at least" (*HC* 3:349).

MAY 10
Choices

Tuesday, 10 May 1836: The Prophet Joseph records: "Brother Heber C. Kimball came to me for counsel, to know whether he should go into the vineyard to proclaim the Gospel, or go to school. I told him he might do either that he should choose, for the Lord would bless him. He chose to go into the vineyard; and immediately went down through the State of New York, into Vermont, his native State. He stopped a short time, and then returned to the city of Ogdensburg, on the St. Lawrence river, where he built up a church of twenty members" (*HC* 2:441). When a faithful brother is faced with a choice between two worthwhile endeavors, the Prophet respects his agency, discerning perhaps that he would decide to do missionary work. Indeed, Brother Kimball selects the missionary option and enjoys immediate success.

MAY 11
Faultfinding

Friday, 11 May 1838: William E. McLellin is brought before a bishop's court in Far West, Missouri, and is excommunicated soon thereafter. Seven years earlier, on August 20, 1831, when he was baptized by Hyrum Smith, William wrote in his journal: "I rose early and betook myself to earnest prayr [sic] to God to direct me into the truth; and from all the light that I could gain by examinations[,] searches and researches I was bound as an honest man to acknowledge the truth and Validity of the Book of Mormon and also that I had found the people of the Lord—The Living Church of Christ" (Susan Easton Black, *Who's Who in the Doctrine & Covenants*, 190). What went wrong? We sense the answer from the council proceedings wherein he stated "that he had no confidence in the heads of the Church, believing they had transgressed, and had got out of the way, consequently he quit praying and keeping the commandments of God, and indulged himself in his lustful desires" (*HC* 3:31).

MAY 12
Every Member to Serve

Sunday, 12 May 1844: Just a month before his martyrdom, the Prophet Joseph Smith is preaching a sermon in Nauvoo in which he makes the following remarkable statement: "Every man who has a calling to minister to the inhabitants of the world was ordained to that very purpose in the Grand Council of heaven before this world was. I suppose that I was ordained to this very office in that Grand Council. . . . The ancient prophets declared that in the last days the God of heaven should set up a kingdom which should never be destroyed. . . . God will always protect me until my mission is fulfilled. I calculate to be one of the instruments of setting up the kingdom of Daniel by the word of the Lord, and I intend to lay a foundation that will revolutionize the whole world" (*HC* 6:364–365). Each and every member has a role to play in this divine process.

MAY 13
Knowledge

Saturday, 13 May 1843: President Joseph Smith and Elders Wilford Woodruff and George A. Smith leave Nauvoo this day for a conference of the Church to be held at "Morley Settlement," or "Yelrome," M-O-R-L-E-Y spelled backwards with an added "e." During the conference the Prophet shares great treasures of knowledge: "The principle of knowledge is the principle of salvation. This principle can be comprehended by the faithful and diligent; and everyone that does not obtain knowledge sufficient to be saved will be condemned. The principle of salvation is given us through the knowledge of Jesus Christ. Salvation is nothing more nor less than to triumph over all our enemies and put them under out feet. And when we have power to put all enemies under our feet in this world, and a knowledge to triumph over all evil spirits in the world to come, then we are saved, as in the case of Jesus, who was to reign until He had put all enemies under His feet, and the last enemy was death" (*HC* 5:387–388).

MAY 14

Abrahamic Covenant

Thursday, 14 May 1840: Joseph Smith pens a letter to Orson Hyde and John E. Page, who were en route to a mission to the Jewish people in Europe and Palestine. Here is a brief excerpt: "If there is anything calculated to interest the mind of the Saints, to awaken in them the finest sensibilities, and arouse them to enterprise and exertion, surely it is the great and precious promises made by our heavenly Father to the children of Abraham; and those engaged in seeking the outcasts of Israel, and the dispersed of Judah, cannot fail to enjoy the Spirit of the Lord and have the choicest blessings of Heaven rest upon them in copious effusions" (*HC* 4:128). Thus the Prophet recalls yet again that the Restoration is in large part due to God remembering His covenants. Orson Hyde dedicated Palestine on Sunday, October 24, 1841, for the return of the Jewish people and the eventual construction of a temple in Jerusalem.

"Abraham received . . . very definite and important covenants that concern us very materially today. . . . One promise was that through him and his seed after him all nations of the earth should be blessed."

(Joseph Fielding Smith, *Doctrines of Salvation*, 3:244, 246)

MAY 15

Aaronic Priesthood

Friday, 15 May 1829: A heavenly messenger—none other than the same John who personally baptized the Savior—descends from the presence of God and, acting under the direction of Peter, James, and John, ordains Joseph Smith and Oliver Cowdery to the Aaronic Priesthood. Of this occasion Oliver writes: "On a sudden, as from the midst of eternity, the voice of the Redeemer spake peace to us, while the veil was parted and the angel of God came down clothed with glory, and delivered the anxiously looked for message, and the keys of the gospel of repentance!—What joy! what wonder! What amazement! While the world were racked and distracted . . . our eyes beheld—our ears heard" (*CHFT*, 55).

MAY 16
Living Scripture

Tuesday, 16 May 1843: On a visit this day to Ramus, a town east of Nauvoo, the Prophet Joseph Smith and one of his travel companions, William Clayton, stay overnight at the home of Benjamin F. Johnson and his wife. Before retiring, the Prophet gives a word of instruction to the Johnsons and Brother Clayton, including this authoritative statement, as recorded in his journal: "In the celestial glory there are three heavens or degrees; and in order to obtain the highest, a man must enter into this order of the priesthood" (*HC* 5:392). This statement is later included in Section 131 of the Doctrine & Covenants (vv. 1–2). The Prophet, trusting in the Lord, continually spoke what amounts to "scripture" in his daily Church service and discourse.

"I feel it a sacred honor . . . to have joined with members of the Church around the world in sustaining the First Presidency and the Quorum of the Twelve Apostles as prophets, seers, and revelators. . . . The Savior said, 'Whether by mine own voice or by the voice of my servants, it is the same' (D&C 1:38)."

(W. Rolfe Kerr, *Ensign,* May 2004, 36)

MAY 17
Knowledge

Wednesday, 17 May 1843: Joseph the Prophet preaches to a gathering of the Saints in Fountain Green, east of Nauvoo. During the evening, the Prophet attends a lecture in Ramus given by a Methodist preacher, and "after [the preacher] got through, [the Prophet] offered some corrections . . ." Joseph then discloses the doctrine in Genesis 2 regarding God breathing the breath of life (spirit) into Adam and Eve, and adds: "There is no such thing as immaterial matter. All spirit is matter, but is more fine or pure, and can only be discerned by purer eyes. We cannot see it, but when our bodies are purified, we shall see that it is all matter" (*HC* 5:392–393). The minister seemed pleased with Joseph's corrections and promised to visit Nauvoo. Many of this day's instructions are included in Section 131.

MAY 18
Prophecy

Thursday, 18 May 1843: The Prophet Joseph Smith dines at Carthage with a young judge of the Illinois Supreme Court, Stephen A. Douglas—at the time a friend of the Saints. During a friendly discussion, the Prophet speaks the following prophetic words: "Judge, you will aspire to the presidency of the United States; and if ever you turn your hand against me or the Latter-day Saints, you will feel the weight of the hand of Almighty upon you; and you will live to see and know that I have testified the truth to you; for the conversation of this day will stick to you through life" (*HC* 5:394). In fulfillment of prophecy, Douglas did indeed run for the presidency, in 1860, but was soundly defeated by Abraham Lincoln. To find the underlying reasons for his disappointment, one need look no further than his refusal to come to the aid of the embattled Saints in Utah. For political reasons he endorsed the lies being perpetrated against the Saints by the enemies of the Church.

MAY 19
The Second Coming

Saturday, 19 May 1838: Joseph Smith and a large company of brethren left Far West, Missouri, yesterday and headed north to find new lands where the Saints could settle. While the group is surveying land nearby called "Spring Hill," Joseph receives a revelation that this same place "by the mouth of the Lord . . . was named Adam-ondi-Ahman, because, said He, it is the place where Adam shall come to visit his people, or the Ancient of Days shall sit, as spoken of by Daniel the Prophet" (*HC* 3:35). In the 1876 edition of the Doctrine & Covenants, Elder Orson Pratt, under the direction of President Brigham Young, included this same revelation, slightly modified, as Section 116 of the Doctrine & Covenants.

"When this gathering is held, the world will not know of it . . . . The Saints cannot know of it—except those who officially shall be called into this council—for it shall precede the coming of Jesus Christ as a thief in the night, unbeknown to all the world."

(Joseph Fielding Smith, *Doctrine & Covenants Student Manual*, 288)

MAY 20

Forgiveness

Friday, 20 May 1842: Joseph Smith sits in a special council in Nauvoo this day to decide the case against Dr. Robert D. Foster, accused of abusive conduct. The Prophet spends considerable time trying to allow Foster repentance rather than excommunication. The Prophet recalls: "I then asked him to tell me where I had done wrong, and I will ask his forgiveness; for I want you to prove to this company by your testimony that I have treated you honorably" (*HC* 6:333). Foster declines to speak and remains irreconcilable, so the Prophet renders this decision: "I then told him I had done my duty; the skirts of my garments were free of his [Foster's] blood; I had made the last overtures of peace to him; and then delivered him into the hands of God" (*HC* 6:345).

"To forgive and forget is an ageless counsel. 'To be wronged or robbed,' said the Chinese philosopher Confucius, 'is nothing unless you continue to remember it.' The injuries inflicted by neighbors, by relatives, or by spouses are generally of a minor nature . . . . We must forgive them."

(Spencer W. Kimball, *Ensign,* Nov. 1977, 48)

MAY 21

Enlightenment

Wednesday, 21 May 1834: Zion's Camp stops for the night just west of Indianapolis. Joseph Smith's journal states: "There had . . . so many reports that we should never be permitted to pass through this place that some of the brethren were afraid that we might have difficulty there. But I had told them in the name of the Lord, we should not be disturbed and that we would pass through . . . without the people knowing it" (*HC* 2:70). These modern Israelites pass unrecognized through the midst of an entire community in fulfillment of the prophecy. The Lord blinds their minds as He did the eyes of Lot's neighbors, the Sodomites (see Gen. 19:11). As the enemies of Zion's Camp were physically blinded, so, too, were they spiritually blind. Spiritual blindness veils the minds of people who refuse to see spiritual truth when it is clearly presented to them (see Jacob 4:14). As the Savior healed the eyes of the physically blind, He is the only conduit for healing the spiritually blind as well.

MAY 22
Friendship

Friday, 22 May 1829: During the month of May, 1829, the Prophet Joseph Smith inquires of the Lord and receives a choice revelation for his loyal friend and erstwhile employer, Joseph Knight, Sr. (now known as Section 12). The older gentleman very much possesses the virtues encouraged in this revelation. Much later, on August 22, 1842, the Prophet recalls with great admiration the friendship of this man: "I contemplate the virtues and the good qualities and characteristics of the faithful few . . . say, for instance, my aged and beloved brother, Joseph Knight, Sen., who was among the number of the first to administer to my necessities, while I was laboring in the commencement of the bringing forth of the work of the Lord. . . . For fifteen years he has been faithful and true, and even-handed and exemplary, and virtuous and kind . . . Behold he is a righteous man, may God Almighty lengthen out the old man's days; and may his trembling, tortured, and broken body be renewed . . ." (*HC* 5:124–125).

MAY 23
Universal Missionary Work

Tuesday, 23 May 1843: Addison Pratt, Noah Rogers, Benjamin Grouard, and Knowlton Hanks are blessed and set apart as the first missionaries to the Pacific Islands. The written minutes of this meeting of the Twelve Apostles report: "President Young said to Brother Addison Pratt and his associates: 'We commit the keys of opening the gospel to the Society Islands to you.' When all the Twelve said, 'Aye,' Elder Rogers was appointed president of the mission" (*HC* 5:405). By late 1846, there are 866 members of the Church from ten branches among the islands in and around Tahiti. Thus the work of the Lord is established in the Pacific (see *CHFT*, 238–239).

"The sun never sets on this work of the Lord as it is touching the lives of people across the earth. . . . We have scarcely scratched the surface."

(Gordon B. Hinckley, *Ensign,* Nov. 2003, 7)

MAY 24
Unity of Purpose

Monday, 24 May 1841: The First Presidency issues a letter, signed by President Joseph Smith, "To the Saints abroad" (meaning outside of Hancock County, Illinois), instructing them to gather to Nauvoo "as soon as circumstances will permit" (*HC* 4:362). The purpose for the call to gather is made clear: "This is important, and should be attended to by all who feel an interest in the prosperity of this corner-stone of Zion. Here the Temple must be raised, the University built, and other edifices erected which are necessary for the great work of the last days, and which can only be done by a concentration of energy and enterprise" (*HC* 4:362). All stakes, except those in Hancock County (Nauvoo) and Lee County (Iowa) are discontinued. Such a concentration of effort around an ultimate purpose is a practice worthy of emulation by all of us today.

"We have a great opportunity . . . to gain the spirit of the gospel as we have never enjoyed it before. This we can do by developing among us that unity required by the laws of the celestial kingdom."

(Marion G. Romney, *Ensign,* May 1983, 18)

MAY 25
Testimony

Monday, 25 May 1829: Samuel H. Smith, the Prophet's next younger brother (21 years of age), is baptized. The Prophet recalls: "About this time my brother . . . came to visit us. We informed him of what the Lord was about to do for the children of men . . . He was not, however, very easily persuaded of these things, but after much inquiry and explanation he retired to the woods, in order that by secret and fervent prayer he might obtain . . . wisdom to . . . judge for himself. The result was that he obtained revelation for himself . . . [and] Oliver Cowdery baptized him; and he returned to his father's house, greatly glorifying and praising God, being filled with the Holy Spirit" (*HC* 1:44). Samuel subsequently becomes one of the Eight Witnesses, who see and handle the gold plates, and the first missionary of the Church.

"Our testimony is a gift from God. It should be shared, but we do not have the authority to bestow a testimony upon someone else, because a personal testimony is granted by the Holy Ghost. [But] it can aid others in gaining knowledge for themselves."

(Robert D. Hales, *New Era,* Aug. 2002, 40)

MAY 26
Reverence for Life

Monday, 26 May 1834: While Zion's Camp is en route to Missouri, the brethren pitching Joseph Smith's tent come across three rattlesnakes. When they attempt to kill the snakes, the Prophet enjoins them with the words: "Let them alone—don't hurt them! How will the serpent ever lose his venom, while the servants of God possess the same disposition, and continue to make war upon it? Men must become harmless, before the brute creation; and when men lose their vicious dispositions and cease to destroy the animal race, the lion and the lamb can dwell together, and the sucking child can play with the serpent in safety" (*HC* 2:71). His listeners carefully remove the snakes on sticks to a place of safety, after which the Prophet exhorts the brethren to kill wildlife only for needful food.

"We do not kill. We are even careful about killing animals, unless we need them for food. . . . Isn't that a terrible thing, to take life just for the fun of it?"

(Spencer W. Kimball, *Teachings of Spencer W. Kimball*, 191)

MAY 27
Joy Despite Death

Wednesday, 27 May 1840: Beloved Bishop Partridge, the first bishop of the Church, dies at age 46. Joseph Smith paid tribute: "He lost his life in consequence of the Missouri persecutions, and he is one of that number whose blood will be required at their hands" (*HC* 4:132). He had earlier characterized Edward Partridge as "a pattern of piety, and one of the Lord's great men" (*HC* 1:128). On January 19th, 1841, the Prophet will receive a revelation with the comforting knowledge that the Lord had received Edward Partridge unto Himself (D&C 124:19). The righteous need not fear death, but rather view it as a joyous event—a release from the cares and sorrows of this arduous, telestial world.

"It is vital to come to an understanding that death is not the end but a new beginning, a necessary stage in our eternal progression."

(Derek A. Cuthbert, *New Era*, Nov. 1985, 48)

MAY 28

Sustaining Church Leaders

❦

Sunday, 28 May 1843: The Prophet Joseph makes this poignant entry in his journal: "Of the Twelve Apostles chosen in Kirtland . . . there have been but two but what have lifted their heel against me" (*HC* 5:412). All of the others, to a greater or lesser degree, at one time or another, had differences with the Prophet or the Church—even Parley P. Pratt. Of his erstwhile disaffection, in May 1837, Parley P. Pratt wrote in his autobiography: "I went to Brother Joseph Smith in tears, and, with a broken heart and contrite spirit, confessed wherein I had erred in spirit, murmured, or done or said amiss. He frankly forgave me, prayed for me and blessed me. Thus, by experience, I learned more fully to discern and to contrast the two spirits, and to resist the one and cleave to the other" (*HC* 2:488).

"Sustaining makes known to the Church who has authority (see D&C 42:11) and enables each of us to show support. We honor all our leaders, both men and women, and are grateful for brothers and sisters so united in this kingdom of God on earth."

(Russell M. Nelson, *Ensign,* Nov. 1989, 20)

MAY 29
Flee Babylon

Monday, 29 May 1843: Brigham Young, under the direction of the First Presidency, publishes the following notice in the *Times & Seasons*: "All the members of [the Philadelphia branch of the Church] who are desirous of doing the will of heaven and of working out their own salvation by keeping the laws of the celestial kingdom, are hereby instructed and counseled to remove from thence without delay and locate themselves in the city of Nauvoo, where God has a work for them to accomplish" (*HC* 5:413).

"The Lord revealed the remedy for . . . spiritual disaster when He counseled Emma Smith to 'lay aside the things of this world, and seek for the things of a better' (D&C 25:10). And Christ provided the pattern, declaring prior to Gethsemane, 'I have *overcome* the world' (John 16:33; emphasis added). The only way that *we* may overcome the world is by coming unto Christ. And coming unto Christ means walking away from the world."

(Sheri L. Dew, *Ensign*, Nov. 1999, 97)

MAY 30
Resourcefulness

Friday, 30 May 1834: The Prophet refers in his journal to a homespun remedy concocted by Ezra Thayre for sick horses in Zion's Camp. With good humor, the Prophet records the recipe: "A three-penny paper of tobacco, half an ounce of copperas [a mineral disinfectant] and two table-spoonsfull of cayenne pepper, and the bottle filled with water when he could not procure whisky. One-half of a bottle constituted a dose, and would almost invariably cure a sick horse in a few minutes, and is worthy of remembrance. Brother Thayre called his medicine '18 by 24'" (*HC* 2:76). This elixir was good evidence of the resourcefulness and practical wisdom among the Saints, and a reminder that the Lord had designated tobacco for medicinal purposes in His "Word of Wisdom," previously given.

MAY 31
Avoiding Greed

Wednesday, 31 May 1837: These are dark days in Kirtland. Sister Eliza R. Snow wrote: "A spirit of speculation had crept into the hearts of [the Saints]. Most of the Saints were poor, and now prosperity was dawning upon them . . . and many who had been humble and faithful to the performance of every duty . . . were getting haughty in their spirits, and lifted up in the pride of their hearts. As the Saints drank in the love and spirit of the world, the Spirit of the Lord withdrew from their hearts" (*HC* 2:487–488). Yet, at this discouraging time (*HC* 2:489), the Lord rejuvenates the Church with an infusion of faithfulness from the humble converts who hungered and thirsted for the gospel.

"The Latter-day Saints who turn their attention to money-making soon . . . . neglect their prayers, become unwilling to pay any donations; the law of tithing gets too great a task for them; and they finally forsake their God, and the providences of heaven seem shut . . . all [due to] lust after the things of this world."

(Brigham Young, *Teachings of Presidents of the Church: Brigham Young,* 237)

JUNE

Build ye houses, and dwell in them;
and plant gardens, and eat the
fruit of them.

—Jer. 29:5

JUNE 1
Obedience

Saturday, 1 Jun. 1833: The Lord first commanded the Saints in December 1832 to build a temple at Kirtland. Six months have elapsed and the construction has still not begun. The Lord gives a strong rebuke in the form of a revelation now found in Section 95. His chastisement refers to such procrastination as "a very grievous sin" (vv. 3, 6). A temple committee is immediately organized, which immediately petitions Church members for every type of assistance. On June 5, George A. Smith hauls the first load of stone while Hyrum Smith and Reynolds Cahoon begin digging the foundation trench for the walls, "and finished the same with their own hands" (*HC* 1:353).

JUNE 2
Creativity

Friday, 2 Jun. 1843: Joseph Smith takes an unusual step to support the travel and the gathering of the Saints. He completes the contract—pending since May 12, 1843—to purchase half interest in the river steamer *Maid of Iowa* (see *HC* 5:386, 417–418). Then he spends the afternoon planning the ensuing day's boat excursion for his family and many friends, including performances by a musical band. The boat was used to ferry people across the Mississippi and also as a means of transporting immigrant Saints arriving in America from England. It would also be used by an expeditionary force attempting to rescue the Prophet when he was arrested the second time (*HC* 5:482–484). The *Maid of Iowa* was finally put up for sale by the Church on April 9, 1845 (*HC* 7:395), thus ending an innovative chapter in the history of the founding of the kingdom of God in our time.

"Creative thinking can become a process of inspiration that leads us to decisions."

(Robert D. Hales, *New Era,* Aug. 1983, 9)

JUNE 3
Bringing Souls to Christ

Friday, 3 Jun. 1831: The fourth general conference of the Church convenes in Kirtland. The office of high priest is conferred for the first time in this dispensation, and many important spiritual truths are conveyed. Church Historian John Whitmer records: "The Spirit of the Lord fell upon Joseph in an unusual manner, and he prophesied that John the Revelator was then among the Ten Tribes of Israel who had been led away by Shalmaneser, king of Assyria, to prepare them for their return from their long dispersion, to again possess the land of their fathers" (*HC* 1:176). As a result of this revelation, we discover that John was at that time performing the work he promised to do—bringing souls to Christ.

"When . . . testimony is born under the inspiration of the Spirit of God, there will be power and a conviction connected with it that will bring souls to Christ, and bringing souls to Christ is our most wonderful privilege."

(Joseph Quinney, Jr., CR, Oct. 1924, 126)

JUNE 4
Stakes of Zion

Tuesday, 4 Jun. 1833: Section 96 is received on the occasion of a conference of high priests in Kirtland (see *HC* 1:352–353). The Lord designates the location for His temple. This revelation, and those immediately preceding it (D&C 94–95) show clearly the Lord's priorities at this time. Second in importance only to the building of the temple is a facility to publish the Lord's word: "This is the most expedient in me, that my word should go forth unto the children of men, for the purpose of subduing the hearts of the children of men for your good" (v. 5). Thus temple attendance and the holy word of God provide the strength of stakes of Zion, then as now.

JUNE 5
Love Your Enemies

Saturday, 5 Jun. 1841: The previous day Joseph Smith called on Governor Thomas Carlin of Illinois while visiting Quincy. Joseph recalls: "I was treated with the greatest kindness and respect" (*HC* 4:364). And yet, on this day, cowardly Governor Carlin dispatches Sheriff Thomas King and a posse to arrest the Prophet on old Missouri matters. The Prophet is then constrained to obtain a writ of habeas corpus to protect himself from the false arrest. The following day, on their return to Nauvoo, Sheriff King was "suddenly seized with sickness." Note the response of a prophet of God: "I nursed and waited upon him in my own house" (*HC* 4:365).

"There is one virtue . . . which, if . . . practiced by the Saints, would prove salvation to thousands upon thousands. I allude to charity . . . ." Never encourage malice or hatred in your hearts; that does not belong to a Saint. . . . Do I say, Love your enemies? Yes, upon certain principles. But you are not required to love their wickedness; you are only required to love them so far as concerns a desire and effort to turn them from their evil ways."

(Brigham Young, *Teachings of Presidents of the Church: Brigham Young*, 217–218)

JUNE 6

Encouragement

Saturday, 6 Jun. 1835: In his journal entry, the Prophet excerpts portions of an article he published in the June issues of *The Messenger and Advocate*, including this gem of instruction for the Elders in Missouri, who had been zealously attending to councils for correcting the Saints: "Instead of trying members for transgression, or offenses [this being the province of the High Council], let every one labor to prepare himself for the vineyard, sparing a little time to comfort the mourners, to bind up the broken-hearted, to reclaim the backslider, to bring back the wanderer . . . and work righteousness, and, with one heart and one mind, prepare to help to redeem Zion, that goodly land of promise, where the willing and obedient shall be blessed" (*HC* 2:229). Thus the Prophet places emphasis on building up, rather than tearing down, the Saints of the Lord.

JUNE 7
Avoid Deception

Tuesday, 7 Jun. 1831: Following an important Church conference that commenced on June 3, several brethren desired to know their duty. In response, about this time, Joseph Smith receives Section 52, wherein the Lord reveals "a pattern in all things, that ye may not be deceived" (D&C 52:14). This two-part pattern includes: (1) *Prayer*— "He that prayeth, whose spirit is contrite, the same is accepted of me if he obey mine ordinances" (v. 15); and (2) *Meekness*— "He that speaketh, whose spirit is contrite, whose language is meek and edifieth, the same is of God if he obey mine ordinances" (v. 16). Those who humbly submit to the Lord's will "shall be made strong, and shall bring forth fruits of praise and wisdom" (v. 17). Obedience is critical in all things (*HC* 1:175–179).

"There is no danger of any man or woman losing his or her faith in this Church if he or she is humble and prayerful and obedient to duty. I have never known of such an individual losing his faith. By doing our duty faith increases until it becomes perfect knowledge."

(Heber J. Grant, *Teachings of Presidents of the Church: Heber J. Grant,* 28)

JUNE 8
Witnesses

Monday, 8 Jun. 1829: In the month of June 1829, the revelation concerning the Three Witnesses to the Book of Mormon is given (D&C 17). After earnest prayer near the Whitmer home in Fayette, New York, and after Martin Harris has removed himself, two of the Three Witnesses are visited by an angel who displays the plates. A voice is heard confirming the truth of the work and commanding those present to "bear record of what you now see and hear" (*HC* 1:55). Soon thereafter Martin Harris, who has sufficiently humbled himself, is also able to participate in the divine manifestation. These three special witnesses uphold the divinity of the Book of Mormon to all the world: "And after that you have obtained faith, and have seen them [the plates] with your eyes, you shall testify of them, by the power of God" (D&C 17:3).

JUNE 9
Mercy

Thursday, 9 Jun. 1842: The Prophet Joseph Smith delivers an address, regarding mercy, to the sisters of the Female Relief Society in Nauvoo. Here is a sampling of his wisdom: "Nothing is so much calculated to lead people to forsake sin as to take them by the hand, and watch over them with tenderness. When persons manifest the least kindness and love to me, O what power it has over my mind, while the opposite course has a tendency to harrow up all the harsh feelings and depress the human mind" (*HC* 5:23–24). And also, "the nearer we get to our Heavenly Father, the more we are disposed to look with compassion on perishing souls; we feel that we want to take them upon our shoulders, and cast their sins behind our backs. . . . If you would have God have mercy on you, have mercy on one another" (*HC* 5:24).

JUNE 10
Persecution

Monday, 10 Jun. 1844: Joseph Smith spends all day in the city council investigating details surrounding the actions of certain individuals "who have formed a conspiracy for the purpose of destroying my life, and scattering the Saints or driving them from the state" (*HC* 6:432). An ordinance is passed concerning libel. Then, under order of the City Council of Nauvoo, the marshal destroys the press that had been used to publish the *Nauvoo Expositor*, a scandal sheet issued on June 7 and sponsored by some of the Church's most bitter and outspoken enemies. This sends a spark into the tinderbox of long-standing enmity against the Church and its leaders. The ensuing chain of legal and mob action leads to the martyrdom of the Prophet and his brother Hyrum on June 27, 1844.

"Think of the early pioneers. . . . Steadfastly they endured—through persecution, expulsion, a governmental order of extermination, expropriation of property, and much more. Their enduring faith in the Lord provided lift for them as it will for you and for me."

(Russell M. Nelson, *Ensign,* May 1997, 70)

JUNE 11
Gathering

Sunday, 11 Jun. 1843: Using the foregoing scripture for his text, Joseph Smith speaks to a large assembly of Saints in Nauvoo on the gathering of Israel: "It was the design of the councils of heaven before the world was that the principles and laws of the priesthood should be predicated upon the gathering of the people in every age of the world. Jesus did everything to gather the people, and they would not be gathered, and He therefore poured out curses upon them. . . . It is for the same purpose that God gathers together His people in the last days, to build unto the Lord a house to prepare them for the ordinances and endowments, washings and anointings, etc." (see *HC* 5:423–424).

"At the commencement of the dispensations God sends out his elders generally to all the world to preach the gospel to every creature. In this dispensation he not only does this; but, as we live in a gathering dispensation, he also gathers in the people."

(John Taylor, *Gospel Kingdom*, 245)

JUNE 12
Melchizedek Priesthood

Friday, 12 Jun. 1829: On the banks of the Susquehanna River, most likely in June 1829, the Melchizedek Priesthood is restored to the earth through the ministration of Peter, James, and John, to the Prophet Joseph Smith and Oliver Cowdery (see D&C 18:9; 20:2–3; 27:12–13; 128:20; *HC* 1:40–42). Only a few weeks earlier, on May 15, 1829, the Aaronic Priesthood was restored under the hands of John the Baptist. Thus the Lord has "committed the keys of my kingdom, and a dispensation of the gospel for the last times . . . in the which I will gather together in one all things" (D&C 27:13).

"When you brethren have an opportunity to exercise the Melchizedek Priesthood, ponder what you are to do. When you lay hands upon the head of another, you are not offering a prayer, which of course requires no authority. You are authorized to set apart, to ordain, to bless, and to speak in the name of the Lord."

(Russell M. Nelson, *Ensign,* Nov. 2003, 46)

JUNE 13
Harmless As Doves

Thursday, 13 Jun. 1844: A meeting is held in nearby Warsaw designed to inflame public sentiment against the Church and its leaders. A written resolution, filled with lies and false accusations, is passed by the group. It begins by condemning violence, but then hypocritically calls for violence against the Saints at Nauvoo (see *HC* 6:462–466). The Saints had previously seen the destruction of their own printing press at Far West, Missouri, to suit the lawless, with no justice ever forthcoming. Similarly, the religious leaders during the time of Christ, whom the Savior labeled hypocrites, trampled on their own voluminous traditional laws to bring about the crucifixion of the Lord. The honest and virtuous subject themselves to law and order while the wicked manipulate or entirely discard law as they please.

"The Savior urged His followers to be 'wise as serpents, and harmless as doves' (Matt. 10:16). . . . Let us so live that if people speak critically of us they must do so falsely and without justification.

(Spencer W. Kimball, *Ensign,* May 1980, 81)

JUNE 14
The Blessing of Health

Wednesday, 14 Jun. 1837: The Prophet Joseph Smith finds himself in excruciating pain from an illness he had contracted on June 12, confining him to his bed at just the time Brigham Young and others were departing for their missions in Great Britain. What the Prophet learns from the experience is noteworthy: "In the midst of it all I felt to rejoice in the salvation of Israel's God, yet I found it expedient to call to my assistance those means which a kind Providence had provided for the restoration of the sick, in connection with the ordinances" (*HC* 2:493). His physician provides herbs and mild food and nurses him back to health. "This is one of the many instances in which I have suddenly been brought from a state of health, to the borders of the grave, and as suddenly restored, for which my heart swells with gratitude to my heavenly Father, and I feel renewedly to dedicate myself and all my powers to His service" (*HC* 2:493).

JUNE 15

Line upon Line

Tuesday, 15 Jun. 1830: During the middle of June 1830, Joseph Smith receives—by revelation—the first of eight chapters comprising the Book of Moses now contained in the Pearl of Great Price. He records: "Amid all the trials and tribulations we had to wade through, the Lord, who well knew our infantile and delicate situation, vouchsafed for us a supply of strength, and granted us 'line upon line of knowledge—here a little and there a little,' of which the following was a precious morsel" (*HC* 1:98). Then follows chapter one of Moses. Within these restored revelations are pearls of great price for all who desire to possess "great knowledge, and to be a greater follower of righteousness," after the manner of Abraham and Moses (see Abr. 1:2).

JUNE 16
Judgment

Monday, 16 Jun. 1834: After the arrival of Zion's Camp in Missouri, amid acute tension between the embattled Saints and the mobbers in Jackson and Clay Counties, the head of one of the most virulent factions, James Campbell, swears an oath against the Mormons: "The eagles and turkey buzzards shall eat my flesh if I do not fix Joe Smith and his army so that their skins will not hold shucks, before two days are passed" (*HC* 2:99). When this group attempts to cross the Missouri River after dark, their boat capsizes, "and the angel of God saw fit to sink the boat about the middle of the river, and seven out of twelve that attempted to cross, were drowned. . . . Campbell was among the missing. He floated down the river some four or five miles, and lodged upon a pile of drift wood, where the eagles, buzzards, ravens, crows, and wild animals ate his flesh from his bones, to fulfil his own words, and left him a horrible example of God's vengeance" (*HC* 2:100).

JUNE 17
Self-Defense

Monday, 17 Jun. 1844: The Prophet Joseph pens a patriotic letter to his Uncle John Smith, reminding his uncle of the rights of the people to defend themselves, stating: "We want this to be your motto in common with us: 'That we will never ground our arms until we give them up by death'" (*HC* 6:486), and then he adds: "It is impossible to give you correct information what to do beforehand; but act according to the emergency of the case, but never give up your arms, but die first" (*HC* 6:486). Joseph had seen the Saints in Missouri surrender their arms to mobs—even to government officials—only to have the mobs return afterward and slaughter innocent, unarmed citizens, as at Haun's Mill.

"There is such a thing as justified self-defense. You have the right to protect yourself against physical harm . . . . You have a right to use physical force to protect virtue, family, freedom. But . . . the righteous only fight as a last resort."

(Larry A. Hiller, *New Era*, Sept. 1997, 42)

JUNE 18
Pray for Safety

Wednesday, 18 Jun. 1834: Toward the end of its trek, Zion's Camp's provisions are exhausted. After a 17-mile march, including wading waist-deep through a slough, they have only cornmeal mush to eat for breakfast. Passing near Richmond, the Prophet Joseph Smith, suffering from illness and fatigue, senses that their location exposes them to attack from enemies. "I almost forgot my sickness, went some distance in the brush, bowed down and prayed my Heavenly Father to suffer no evil to come upon us, but keep us safe through the night. I obtained an assurance that we should be safe until morning" (*HC* 2:102). They are indeed protected throughout the night.

"Our prayers . . . should be focused on the . . . everyday struggles of life. . . . Instead of worrying, focus on doing all that you can, and then leave the worrying to your Heavenly Father. . . . My mother and father gathered the family to kneel in prayer morning and night and pled for my safety. I know that I felt the influence of those prayers. . . . I trusted . . . that He would preserve my life."

(Joseph B. Wirthlin, *Ensign,* Mar. 2004, 26–29)

JUNE 19

Justice of God

Thursday, 19 Jun. 1834: Under certain conditions God declares that He will fight the Saints' battles for them. This pertains this day. A mob of nearly 400 men are converging upon the Saints' location. Five scouts from the mob visit the camp, threatening that the Mormons will "see hell before morning" (*HC* 2:103). Some of the brethren desire to fight, but Joseph tells them, "Stand still, and see the salvation of God" (*CHFT,* 148; cf. Ex. 14:13). Wilford Woodruff records what appeared in the hitherto-clear skies moments after the scouts' departure: "A small cloud like a black spot appeared in the north west, and it began to unroll itself like a scroll, and in a few minutes the whole heavens were covered with a pall as black as ink" (*HC* 2:104). The ensuing storm, of unprecedented violence, entirely frustrates the schemes of the scattering mob. Joseph declares, "God is in this storm." The surviving mobocrats decide that "when Jehovah fights they would rather be absent" (*HC* 2:102).

JUNE 20
Loyalty

Tuesday, 20 Jun. 1843: The Prophet mentions a report "of various persons in Great Britain and Ireland" who contributed toward building the temple. "The names of the donors and amounts are recorded in the 'Law of the Lord'" (*HC* 5:438). He kept a special book called "the Book of the Law of the Lord" in which he recorded the names of people "such as have stood by me in every hour of peril" (*HC* 5:124). Some honorable mentions include his parents, Joseph Knight, Sr. (with sons Newel and Joseph, Jr.), and Orrin Porter Rockwell. "There is a numerous host of faithful souls, whose names I could wish to record in the Book of the Law of the Lord; but time and chance would fail" (*HC* 5:125).

"Will you all stand by me to the death, and sustain at the peril of your lives, the laws of our country . . . ? ('Aye!' shouted thousands) . . . You are a good people; therefore I love you with all my heart. . . . You have stood by me in the hour of trouble, and I am willing to sacrifice my life for your preservation."

(Joseph Smith, *HC* 6:499–500)

JUNE 21
Peace

Friday, 21 Jun. 1844: Governor Thomas Ford of Illinois has arrived in Carthage. He sends a messenger to deliver a letter to Mayor Joseph Smith and the Nauvoo City Council requesting that they dispatch some "well-informed and discreet persons" to meet him who are "capable of laying before me your [the Church's] version of the matter" that has caused what Governor Ford perceives as almost certain civil war between the Saints and their enemies (*HC* 6:521). Men return to the governor, bearing a wide variety of written affidavits and testimonies, together with a letter from Joseph Smith. In spite of the Saints' overtures for peace and the Prophet's attempts at quelling strife, it is clear that the governor has already been persuaded that the Saints are the guilty party and breakers of the peace.

"Peace does not come to the transgressor of law; peace comes by obedience to law, and it is that message which Jesus would have us proclaim among men."

(David O. McKay, CR, Oct. 1938, 133)

JUNE 22
Patience

Sunday, 22 Jun. 1834: The extraordinary "Fishing River" revelation (Section 105) is given shortly after the arrival of Zion's Camp in Missouri (see *HC* 2:108–111). The Lord chastens the Church: "Behold, I say unto you, were it not for the transgressions of my people, speaking concerning the church and not individuals, they might have been redeemed even now" (v. 2). As it is, the Lord counsels his elders to "wait for a little season for the redemption of Zion," until after they are "endowed with power from on high" (v. 9, 11). Nevertheless, the faithful are to be blessed for their offering: "It is expedient in me that they should be brought thus far for a trial of their faith" (v. 19). Saints of today, studying this revelation, can gain insight into the timetable of the Lord as He teaches His Saints the principles of patience, obedience, and sacrifice.

JUNE 23
Self-Sacrifice

Sunday, 23 Jun. 1844: Daybreak finds Joseph and Hyrum Smith on the Iowa bank of the Mississippi River, having rowed all night aboard a leaky skiff to avoid arrest by Governor Ford's posse. Reynolds Cahoon joins Joseph in Iowa with a letter asking Joseph to return and surrender to the authorities; some fear that he is abandoning the Church, and they importune him to remain and prevent its destruction. Joseph responds: "If my life is of no value to my friends it is of none to myself" (*HC* 6:549). Addressing Hyrum, who has counseled that they return, he says: "If you go back I will go with you, but we shall be butchered" (*HC* 6:549–550). During the return journey, the Prophet utters his immortal words: "I am going like a lamb to the slaughter, but I am calm as a summer's morning. I have a conscience void of offense toward God and toward all men" (*HC* 6:555).

JUNE 24
Obedience

Tuesday, 24 Jun. 1834: This is the last full day of Zion's Camp in Missouri before it is disbanded into smaller groups and dispersed. The Prophet warned them that murmuring and lack of commitment would bring the Lord's retribution. As a result, an outbreak of cholera reaches its "most virulent form" during the night (*HC* 2:114). In connection with this, the Prophet learns a great lesson: "At the commencement, I attempted to lay on hands for their recovery, but I quickly learned by painful experience, that when the great Jehovah decrees destruction upon any people . . . man must not attempt to stay His hand. The moment I attempted to rebuke the disease I was attacked, and had I not desisted in my attempt to save the life of a brother, I would have sacrificed my own." Nearly seventy are stricken by the disease, including the Prophet, and fourteen die before the members covenant to obey the Lord's counsel (*HC* 2:114–120).

JUNE 25

Pure Doctrine

Tuesday, 25 Jun. 1833: Joseph Smith and the First Presidency write a letter to the Church leaders in Zion (Missouri). It is apparent that someone in Far West had been teaching that Satan and his followers would one day be forgiven of their rebellion and redeemed. In response, the Presidency counsels: "The Lord never authorized them to say that the devil, his angels or the sons of perdition, should ever be restored; for their state of destiny was not revealed to man, is not revealed, nor ever shall be revealed, save to those who are made partakers thereof [see D&C 76:30–49]: consequently those who teach this doctrine, have not received it of the Spirit of the Lord" (*HC* 1:366).

JUNE 26
Testimony

Wednesday, 26 Jun. 1844: On the eve of his martyrdom, the Prophet Joseph Smith prophesies and bears witness of the gospel of Jesus Christ. Assisted by his brother Hyrum and other associates, he preaches to the guards, several of whom leave their post early because they are convinced of the innocence of their prisoners (see *HC* 6:592). Joseph bears a powerful testimony to the guards "that the kingdom of God was again established upon the earth" (*HC* 6:600).

"Of the many examples recorded of his loving nature . . . [one] occurred in Carthage Jail the night before [Joseph's] death. . . . [Here] his heart turned outward to comfort someone else. When all were apparently fast asleep, Joseph whispered to Dan Jones, are you afraid to die? Dan [answered], Has that time come, think you? Engaged in such a cause I do not think that death would have many terrors. Joseph replied, You will yet see Wales, and fulfill the mission appointed you before you die.'"

(Henry B. Eyring, *Ensign*, Nov. 2003, 91–92)

JUNE 27
Martyrdom

Tuesday, 27 Jun. 1844: In the morning, Joseph Smith writes to his wife Emma from Carthage Jail: "Dear Emma, I am very much resigned to my lot, knowing I am justified, and have done the best that I could. Give my love to the children and all my friends" (*HC* 6:605). Elder Taylor later states: "To seal the testimony of this book [the Doctrine & Covenants] and the Book of Mormon, we announce the martyrdom of Joseph Smith the Prophet, and Hyrum Smith the Patriarch" (D&C 135:11). The Lord Himself memorialized the man Joseph Smith, "whom I did call upon by mine angels . . . by mine own voice . . . to bring forth my work; Which foundation he did lay, and was faithful; and I took him to myself. Many have marveled because of his death; but it was needful that he should seal his testimony with his blood, that he might be honored and the wicked might be condemned" (D&C 136:37–39).

JUNE 28
The Second Coming

Thursday, 28 Jun. 1838: The Prophet presides over a special conference held at Adam-ondi-Ahman, Missouri (*HC* 3:38–40). The Saints flock to this community in large numbers all summer, honored to live at the place where Adam once dwelt (D&C 78:15–16; 107:53). It will be to this same place that Adam will one day return for a grand council at which the Savior Himself will preside over the gathering in of all keys of the priesthood on the eve of His millennial reign (D&C 116; 128:21). Thus, on June 28, 1838, the Saints are taking important steps to prepare themselves for the Second Coming; we, at the turn of the new millennium, are closer still to that long-heralded event.

JUNE 29
Knowing God

Monday, 29 Jun. 1829: In a concise reference to eternal life, John recorded Jesus' words to His Father during His great intercessory prayer: "And this is life eternal, that they might know thee the only true God, and Jesus Christ, whom thou hast sent" (John 17:3). Yet how do we come to really know Him? "Beloved, let us love one another . . . and every one that loveth is born of God, and knoweth God" (1 John 4:7). Additionally John tells us: "And hereby we do know that we know him, if we keep his commandments" (1 John 2:3). Joseph Smith provides another key for how to know God, which he received directly from heaven in June 1829: "These words are not of men nor of man, but of me. . . . Wherefore, you can testify that you have heard my voice, and know my words" (D&C 18:34–36).

"There is a great difference in believing or knowing that there is a God and in knowing God. When we claim that we know God, . . . there is great responsibility to respect and love and follow his counsel and his doctrines and his commandments and to grow as a child to become more godlike."

(Bernard P. Brockbank, *Ensign,* Jul. 1972, 121–122)

JUNE 30
Friendship

Friday, 30 Jun. 1843: Joseph Smith arrives in triumph in Nauvoo after his enemies have failed for a third time to extradite him to Missouri on a trumped-up charge of treason—lawmen having attempted to arrest him while he was visiting family away from Nauvoo. "After embracing Emma and my brother Hyrum, who wept tears of joy at my return, as did also most of the great company who surrounded us, . . . I mounted my favorite horse, 'Old Charley,' when the band struck up 'Hail Columbia,' and proceeded to march slowly towards the city, Emma riding by my side into town. . . . The multitude seemed unwilling to disperse until after I had arisen on the fence and told them, 'I am out of the hands of the Missourians again, thank God. I thank you all for you kindness and love to me" (*HC* 5:459).

"Among life's sweetest blessings is fellowship with men and women whose ideals and aspirations are high and noble. . . . Friendship is a sacred possession. As air, water, and sunshine to flowers, trees, and verdure, so smiles, sympathy, and love of friends to the daily life of man!"

(David O. McKay, *Gospel Ideals*, 253)

JULY

[Those] willing to observe their covenants by sacrifice . . . are accepted of me."

—D&C 97:8

JULY 1
Peace

Monday, 1 Jul. 1844: In the aftermath of the martyrdom of Joseph and Hyrum, Governor Ford and local authorities are extremely anxious about a "Mormon" uprising against the perpetrators, and have urged Church officials to pacify the Saints in favor of peace. W.W. Phelps, Willard Richards, and John Taylor today issue an "Address to the Church of Jesus Christ of Latter-day Saints—A Word of Consolation." This proclamation proposes guidelines which may be wisely employed by Saints on a quest for peace today: "Be peaceable, quiet citizens, doing the works of righteousness. . . . The righteous blood of all the holy Prophets . . . only carries conviction to the bosoms of all intelligent beings, that the cause is just and will continue. . . . Union is peace, brethren, and eternal life is the greatest gift of God (*HC* 7:152–153).

JULY 2
Humility

Tuesday, 2 Jul. 1839: In Montrose, Iowa (across the river from Nauvoo), the Prophet Joseph Smith counsels the Twelve and some of the Seventy prior to their departure to Europe. His theme is guarding against "self-sufficiency, self-righteousness, and self-importance" (*HC* 3:383). He gives them the touchstones of compliance—a willingness to confess their sins, forgive others, and remain humble. Moreover, they should "not seek to excel one above another, but act for each other's good, and pray for one another, and honor our brother or make honorable mention of his name, and not backbite and devour our brother." When they excel at preaching the gospel and evoke the admiration of their listeners, they are to "ascribe the praise and glory to God and the Lamb," rather than to themselves, for "from whom receivest thou thy power and blessings, but from God?" (*HC* 3:384).

JULY 3
Apathy

Friday, 3 Jul. 1840: The Saints have repeatedly petitioned Congress, the president, and numerous state and county civil authorities for redress for the wrongs they have suffered at the hands of fierce mobs in Missouri and elsewhere. Joseph records some of his reflections regarding the apathy of the government: "Since Congress has decided against us, the Lord has begun to vex this nation, and He will continue to do so except they repent; for they now stand guilty . . . because they have refused to protect their citizens" (*HC* 4:145). The implication of the Prophet's words is clear: If this nation should continue to turn an indifferent eye to justice and to God, the day would arrive when peace would again be taken from this country and "war will be poured out upon all nations" (D&C 87:2).

"Edmund Burke once said, 'All that is necessary for the triumph of evil is for good men to do nothing.' . . . We must become responsible citizens and carry out our civic duty."

(Ezra Taft Benson, *Teachings of Ezra Taft Benson*, 676–677)

JULY 4
Independence

Tuesday, 4 Jul. 1843: Some 15,000 gather in the grove near the Nauvoo Temple to celebrate Independence Day and listen to the Prophet speak. Solemnly declaring his innocence of the charges of treason currently pending against him in Missouri, he expresses his determination to submit to the will of God. "All the power that I desire or have sought to obtain has been the enjoyment of the constitutional privilege for which my fathers shed their blood, of living in peace in the society of my wife and children, and enjoying the society of my friends and that religious liberty which is the right of every American citizen, of worshiping according to the dictates of his conscience and the revelations of God" (*HC* 5:489–490). Thus the Prophet sets the stage for this day of festivities accompanied by jubilation, band music, and cannon fire.

JULY 5
Infamy

Friday, 5 Jul. 1844: "Mr. Daniels started about 9 A.M. to . . . tell [the governor] what he knew in relation to the massacre of the Generals Smith" (*HC* 7:168). William Daniels' sympathetic views of the prophetic calling of Joseph Smith did not please Governor Ford. In his *History of Illinois,* the governor records an almost prophetic reflection of how history may perceive himself and Joseph Smith in light of his (Ford's) official connection with the martyrdom. Ford writes: "It is to be feared that in course of the century, some gifted man . . . may . . . make the name of the martyred Joseph ring as loud, and stir the souls of men as much, as the mighty name of Christ itself. . . . And in that event, the author of this *History* feels degraded by the reflection, that the humble governor of an obscure state stands a fair chance, like Pilate . . . of being dragged down to posterity with an immortal name, hitched on to the memory of a miserable impostor" (*HC* 7:40–41).

"I wish not to be critical of Governor Ford. I feel sorry for him. I regard him as one who sowed the wind and reaped the whirlwind."

(Gordon B. Hinckley, *Ensign,* May 1994, 73–74

JULY 6
Obedience

Friday, 6 Jul. 1838: The "Kirtland Camp" of some 529 Saints (105 families) commences the 870-mile trek from Kirtland to Far West and on to Adam-ondi-Ahman, Missouri. Organized and directed by the Seventies in response to the commandment of the Lord to remove to Zion (D&C 58:56), this company displays singular faithfulness. The chronicle of this journey (*HC* 3:87–148) is a blend of opposites: tedious routines and exciting adventure, unity of the many and disaffection of the few, followership and leadership, sickness and health, birth and death, sorrow and joy, accident and divine intervention.

"You will remember when Adam was driven from the Garden of Eden he offered sacrifices. 'An angel of the Lord appeared unto Adam, saying: Why dost thou offer sacrifices unto the Lord? And Adam said unto him: I know not, save the Lord commanded me' (Moses 5:6). Then the angel explained to him the meaning of sacrifices. Obedience must always precede knowledge. If we are obedient to our assigned responsibility, knowledge will follow."

(Howard W. Hunter, *The Teachings of Howard W. Hunter*, 22)

JULY 7
Conversion

Sunday, 7 Jul. 1839: A large group assembles at Commerce (Nauvoo), Illinois, to listen to farewell addresses by the Twelve Apostles, who are about to leave on their missions to the nations of the earth. Many in the congregation are not members of the Church; therefore, the brethren bear strong witness of the divinity of the Restoration, and in particular of the Book of Mormon. Apostle John E. Page emphasizes that no impostor would dare to make promises such as are contained in the Book of Mormon, by which readers could know of its truth through study, prayer, and spiritual confirmation.

"I [have] learned this one fact, that you might prove doctrine from the Bible till doomsday, and it would merely convince a people, but would not convert them. . . . Nothing short of a testimony by the power of the Holy Ghost would bring light and knowledge to them . . . You have frequently heard me say that I would rather hear an Elder . . . speak only five words accompanied by the power of God, and they would do more good than to hear long sermons without the Spirit."

(Brigham Young, *Teachings of Presidents of the Church: Brigham Young,* 246)

JULY 8
Tithing

Sunday, 8 Jul. 1838: On this Sunday, the Prophet Joseph Smith inquires of the Lord, "O Lord! Show unto thy servant how much thou requirest of the properties of thy people for a tithing" (*HC* 3:44). He then receives Sections 119 and 120, providing the law of tithing. The Lord commands the Saints of that time to make two kinds of payments: first, "all their surplus property," and secondly, "one-tenth of all their interest annually" (D&C 119:1–4). The spiritual purpose of tithing is "to prepare [the Saints] against the day of vengeance and burning" (D&C 85:3).

"The First Presidency has written what the law of tithing is for us today: 'The simplest statement we know of is the statement of the Lord himself, namely, that the members of the Church should pay "one tenth of all their interest annually," which is understood to mean income. No one is justified in making any other statement than this' (First Presidency letter, 19 March 1970)."

(Robert D. Hales, *Ensign,* Dec. 1986, 17)

JULY 9
An Acceptable Offering

Friday, 9 Jul. 1841: On July 1, Brigham Young, now President of the Quorum of the Twelve, returned to Nauvoo with Heber C. Kimball and John Taylor, having spent the previous two years serving the Lord in England. Now, in President Young's own home, the Prophet Joseph receives a comforting revelation on his behalf (Section 126), informing Brigham that he will no longer need to leave his family for long-term or long-distance missions (see *HC* 4:382). President Young, like most of the early Church leaders, performed numerous distant missions for the Church and spent a great deal of time away from his family.

"Shortly after the return of the Twelve, Joseph stated . . . that the time had come when the Apostles must stand in their places next to the First Presidency. They had been faithful and had borne the burden and heat of the day, giving the gospel triumph in the nations of the earth, and it was right that they should now remain at home and perform the duty in Zion."

(George Q. Cannon, In Roy W. Doxey, *Latter-day Prophets and the Doctrine and Covenants,* 4:305)

JULY 10
Music

Saturday, 10 Jul. 1830: Sometime during the month of July, 1830, soon after the organization of the Church, the Prophet receives a revelation (Section 25) for Emma, his wife (see *HC* 1:103–104). She is given a full array of responsibilities, among which is to make a selection of sacred hymns for the Church. It is in relation to this last task that the Lord gives the famous passage in Section 25 (v. 12) concerning His delight in edifying music.

"No individual singer, or organization of singers, in the Church, should ever render a selection unless the words are in full harmony with the truths of the gospel, and can be given from the heart of the singer. In other words, our songs should be in very deed 'prayers unto the Lord' [see D&C 25:12]. If we are careful to sing only such songs, then we are sure of the blessings which are promised by the Lord, because his promises are 'true and faithful and will all be fulfilled' [see D&C 1:37]."

(Heber J. Grant, *Teachings of Presidents of the Church: Heber J. Grant*, 167)

JULY 11
Missionary Work

Saturday, 11 Jul. 1840: William Barrett, age 17, from Staffordshire, England, is ordained an elder and called to serve as the first missionary to Australia (*HC* 4:154). Elder Barrett wastes no time, and the following April, he reports from Adelaide, Australia, that "obstacles to the introduction of the work of the Lord are very great" (*HC* 4:343). In 1921, when David O. McKay visited Australia on apostolic assignment, the number of Saints in the land down under were still few, yet Elder McKay "detected deep spirituality among the people" (*CHFT*, 501). Today, Australia, which began as a British penal colony, numbers many stakes and numerous warm-hearted and strong Saints.

"Even the anticipation of bringing souls to Christ can make one happy. Alma demonstrated this while teaching the words of Christ to a group of apostate Nephites. When the poverty-stricken Zoramites began asking him gospel-related questions, 'he turned him about . . . and he beheld with great joy . . . that they were in a preparation to hear the word' (Alma 32:6."

(David M. Whitchurch, *Ensign*, Aug. 2000, 35)

JULY 12
Eternal Marriage

Wednesday, 12 Jul. 1843: The Prophet Joseph Smith dictates to his scribe, William Clayton, in the presence of Hyrum Smith, the great revelation on eternal marriage, likely first revealed to the Prophet in 1831. In scope of theme and grandeur of language, this revelation is unsurpassed in all of holy writ. This law (also set forth in Section 131) is an indispensable part of the Abrahamic Covenant: "Go ye, therefore, and do the works of Abraham; enter ye into my law and ye shall be saved" (v. 32; see also *HC* 5:xxix–xlvi; 500–507).

"The 'New and Everlasting Covenant,' referred to in . . . section 132, is the covenant of celestial and eternal marriage "*new*" to this dispensation, being a matrimonial union for time and all eternity, whereas marriage as previously understood and solemnized in the world was simply until the pair were parted by death. . . . Celestial marriage is essential to a fullness of glory in the world to come, as explained in the revelation concerning it, but it is not stated that plural marriage is thus essential."

(Charles W. Penrose, *Improvement Era,* 15:1042)

JULY 13
Church Publications

Friday, 13 Jul. 1832: Joseph Smith writes: "In July, we received the first number of *The Evening and Morning Star*, which was a joyous treat to the Saints. Delightful, indeed, was it to contemplate that the little band of brethren had become so large . . . as to be able to issue a paper of their own . . . which would gratify and enlighten the humble inquirer after truth" (*HC* 1:273). A conference the previous fall determined that W.W. Phelps should purchase a printing press to publish a Church newspaper at Far West. Part of his prospectus on the purpose of the publication states, "Therefore, in the fear of Him [the Lord], and to spread the truth among all nations, kindreds, tongues and people, this paper is sent forth, that a wicked world may know that Jesus Christ, the Redeemer, who shall come to Zion will soon appear" (*HC* 1:259).

"I really believe that anyone who contributes to the circulation of . . . [Church magazines] is blessing the people. We do not read enough and we do not read enough of the right kind of literature."

(John A. Widstoe, in Alan K. Parrish, *John A. Widstoe: A Biography,* 558)

JULY 14
Endurance

Sunday, 14 Jul. 1833: During the month of July, a secret document is circulated among mob members in Jackson County, Missouri. This "Manifesto of the Mob" lays out a rationale and strategy for ridding the state of the Saints, "peaceably if we can, forcibly if we must" (*HC* 1:374). They set forth objections to Church doctrines, such as continuing revelation and spiritual gifts, and accuse the Saints of being idle, poverty-stricken, and of fomenting dissension among the slaves. Hundreds sign the conspiratorial document, which is read before a large gathering of mobbers at the Independence Courthouse on July 20. Mobs then destroy the W.W. Phelps home and printing office and cause Bishop Edward Partridge and a young eastern convert, when they refuse to recant their testimonies, to be tarred and feathered. Fortunately, though mobs destroyed the printing office, two heroic young girls are able to save a few unbound copies of the "Book of Commandments" (the predecessor to the Doctrine & Covenants), then at Phelps' press.

JULY 15
Government

Friday, 15 Jul. 1842: An instructive article appears in the *Times & Seasons*, entitled "The Government of God." It provides contrast between God's method of governing and men's, proposing that if men apply godly principles within their laws and administrations, those nations will prosper, as did Egypt under Joseph. The article asserts: "The government of God has always tended to promote peace, unity, harmony, strength, and happiness; while that of man has been productive of confusion, disorder, weakness, and misery" (*HC* 5:61).

"We urge our members to do their civic duty and to assume their responsibilities as individual citizens in seeking solutions to the problems which beset our cities and communities. With our wide-ranging mission, so far as mankind is concerned, Church members cannot ignore the many practical problems that require solution if our families are to live in an environment conducive to spirituality."

(Ezra Taft Benson, *This Nation Shall Endure*, 78–79)

JULY 16
Looking Within

Sunday, 16 Jul. 1843: The Prophet Joseph Smith preaches in the morning and evening in the large grove to the west of the Nauvoo Temple. His subject: "A man's foes being those of his own household" (*HC* 5:510). At a time when the Church is beset by threats and violence from without, the Prophet reminds his flock that the real enemies are within. "The same spirit that crucified Jesus is in the breast of some who profess to be Saints in Nauvoo," he declares. His purpose was to encourage the spirit of cleansing from within. We should look within our own sphere, beginning with ourselves, then our own family and immediate circle of associates, in order to purify Zion.

"We have those in the Church these days, as there were in Nauvoo, who profess membership but spend much of their time . . . looking for defects in the Church, in its leaders, in its programs. They contribute nothing to the building of the kingdom. They rationalize their efforts . . . but the result of those efforts is largely only a fragmentation of faith, their own and that of others."

(Gordon B. Hinckley, *Teachings of Gordon B. Hinckley*, 121–122)

JULY 17
Magnify Your Office

Tuesday, 17 Jul. 1832: The second issue of the new Church publication, the *Evening & Morning Star,* appeared this month. Editor W.W. Phelps prints some inspiring articles for the Saints to read. Here are some excerpts: "Brethren . . . You are to walk in the valley of humility, and pray for the salvation of all; yes, you are to pray for your enemies; and warn in compassion without threatening. . . . You are the light of the world in matters of pure religion, and many souls may be required at you hands. Let the idea not leave you, that not only the eyes of the world, but the eyes of the angels and of God are upon you" (*HC* 1:280–81).

"President John Taylor warned us: 'If you do not magnify your calling, God will hold you responsible for those whom you might have saved had you done your duty'. . . . If great joy is the reward of saving one soul, then how terrible must be the remorse of those whose timid efforts have allowed a child of God to go unwarned or unaided so that he has to wait till a dependable servant of God comes along.'"

(Thomas S. Monson, *Ensign,* May 1992, 48)

JULY 18
Gardening

Tuesday, 18 Jul. 1843: "I was making hay on my farm." This one-sentence entry from Joseph Smith's journal (*HC* 5:511) is a reminder that this great prophet, statesman, military officer, writer, poet, teacher, colonizer, and city-builder is also rooted in the soil and aware of the obligation to feed his family. No doubt this strenuous physical activity is a soothing respite from the pressures of his office. It may also give an opportunity to meditate and think upon the future—one that for him would last less than a year more in its mortal phase.

"We have urged you to plant gardens and trees. . . . We are sure that you have reduced, to some extent, the high cost of living by having these fresh vegetables. . . . The Lord said, as He planted a garden in Eden, 'All things which I prepared for the use of man; and man saw that it was good for food' (Moses 3:8–9). 'And I, the Lord God, took the man, and put him into the Garden of Eden, to dress it, and to keep it' (Moses 3:15)."

(Spencer W. Kimball, *Ensign,* Nov. 1975, 5)

JULY 19
Faith

Saturday, 19 Jul. 1828: About this time in July, the Prophet receives Section 3, "relating to the lost 116 pages of manuscript translated from the first part of the Book of Mormon" (Preamble). Joseph had reluctantly given in to the insistent requests of Martin Harris to borrow the early portion of the translation, which was subsequently lost. Now the Prophet is firmly chastised for that transgression and for "fear[ing] man more than God" (D&C 3:7; see also D&C 10; *HC* 1:20–31). It appears to be a simple matter of faith, for the Lord promises that if we are faithful He will support us against temptation and be with us in every time of trouble. Moreover, if we "rely upon the merits of Jesus Christ," we will be "glorified through faith in his name" (v. 20).

"Fear is the antithesis of faith. . . . 'For God hath not given us the spirit of fear; but of power, and of love, and of a sound mind' [2 Tim. 1:7]. . . . We need not fear as long as we have in our lives the *power* that comes from righteously living by the truth which is from God our Eternal Father. Nor need we fear as long as we have the *power of faith.*"

(Gordon B. Hinckley, *Ensign,* Oct. 1984, 2–4)

JULY 20

Valor

Saturday, 20 Jul. 1833: Bishop Edward Partridge is tarred and feathered by mobbers in Independence, Missouri. Before suffering this painful abuse, Bishop Partridge is permitted to speak: "I told them that the Saints had suffered persecution in all ages of the world; that I had done nothing which ought to offend anyone; that if they abused me, they would abuse an innocent person; that I was willing to suffer for the sake of Christ. . . . I bore my abuse with so much resignation and meekness, that it appeared to astound the multitude, who permitted me to retire in silence, many looking very solemn, their sympathies having been touched as I thought; and as to myself, I was so filled with the Spirit and love of God, that I had no hatred toward my persecutors or anyone else" (*HC* 1:391).

JULY 21
Truth

Tuesday, 21 Jul. 1835: Earlier this month Michael H. Chandler had brought four mummies and some ancient scrolls to Kirtland as part of a traveling museum. The Prophet bought the scrolls and began translating the hieroglyphics found on them, and he discovered with joy that they contained the Book of Abraham and the Book of Joseph of Egypt. "Truly we can say," he reports, "the Lord is beginning to reveal the abundance of peace and truth" (*HC* 2:236). With the help of scribes, and through weeks of analysis and careful research, Joseph also assembles an alphabet relating to the materials that have come into his hands. The reward is clear: "During the research, the principles of astronomy as understood by Father Abraham and the ancients unfolded to our understanding" (*HC* 2:286).

JULY 22

Power of God

Monday, 22 Jul. 1839: This was termed by Wilford Woodruff the "greatest day for the manifestation of the power of God through the gift of healing since the organization of the Church" (*CHFT*, 218–219). Thousands of Saints had arrived in Nauvoo unaware of the dangers from malaria-bearing mosquitoes in the undrained swamplands. Hundreds contract the disease, including the Prophet, and great numbers are dying. The Prophet, moved by the Spirit, rises up from his sick bed and begins administering to the ill, healing many in a marvelous manifestation of the power of God (see *HC* 4:3–5). In one especially poignant incident, a nonmember traveler from the West, who has witnessed the miraculous events of the day, beckons the Prophet to come and heal his stricken three-month-old twins. The Prophet is unable to go back the two miles to the bedside of the children, so he takes from his pocket a silk handkerchief and gives it to Wilford Woodruff with the instructions to use it to wipe the faces of the children, promising that they will be healed. They were healed as promised.

JULY 23
Humility

Sunday, 23 Jul. 1837: Heber C. Kimball, Orson Hyde, and other missionaries called to Great Britain give the first sermons in that land and thus launch the extraordinary process of gathering the receptive and humble from among the people (*HC* 2:498–499). In Kirtland, Joseph Smith receives Section 112 on behalf of Thomas B. Marsh, who is the President of the Quorum of the Twelve Apostles at this time. The Lord instructs Elder Marsh in a way that can be applied to our own lives. Amid a message that the gospel is to go forth, admonitions are given for humility (vv. 3, 10, 21–22) and readiness for "a day of wrath" (v. 24). "Cleanse your hearts and your garments, lest the blood of this generation be required at your hands" (v. 33). If we begin to emulate the world, we will be the first to feel of His impending wrath: "And upon my house shall it begin, and from my house shall it go forth, saith the Lord" (v. 25).

JULY 24

A Promised Land

Saturday, 24 Jul. 1847: Just over three years after the martyrdom of the Prophet Joseph Smith, Brigham Young and his stalwart company of pioneers reach the Salt Lake Valley, where he utters his now famous statement, "It is enough. This is the right place. Drive on" (*CHFT*, 333). At last the Saints had reached a dwelling place where they could establish themselves as a mighty people and move into the next phase of growth for the kingdom of God on the earth. The seeds first planted by Joseph and sealed with the martyrs' blood could germinate in soil where the fruits of peace, unity, and obedience could flourish unhampered by the persecutor.

"If we had Brother George A. Smith to tell the story, he would say we came here because we were obliged to come, and we stay here because there is no other place to which we can go. . . . The people have hardly commenced to realize the beauty, excellence, and glory that will yet crown this city. I do not know that I will live in the flesh to see what I saw in vision when I came here."

(Brigham Young, *Journal of Discourses,* 12:93–94)

JULY 25
Neighborly Relations

Monday, 25 Jul. 1836: After their expulsion from Jackson County, Missouri, in 1833, the impoverished Saints remained primarily in Caldwell County, where citizens had initially welcomed them with sympathetic arms. However, as days pass into months and as numerous new Saints arrive daily, the citizens' patience with the Mormons begins to wear thin. Requests are made for them to move on. As tensions with the "old settlers" escalate, Joseph Smith and other leaders in Kirtland write to Church authorities in Missouri: "You have thus far had an asylum, and now seek another, as God may direct. . . . Be wise; let prudence dictate all your counsels; preserve peace with all men, if possible; stand by the Constitution of your country; observe its principles; and above all, show yourselves men of God" (*HC* 2:455).

JULY 26
God's Word

Monday, 26 Jul. 1830: In the month of July, after receiving the revelations in the Doctrine & Covenants, Sections 24, 25, and 26, the Prophet Joseph Smith is saddened to receive a letter from Oliver Cowdery criticizing some of the text of the revelation (see *HC* 1:105). "I immediately wrote to him in reply," says the Prophet, "in which I asked him by what authority he took upon him to command me to alter . . . add to or diminish from, a revelation or commandment from Almighty God." A few days later he visits Oliver and convinces him by reason and scripture study. "And thus was this error rooted out . . . to teach . . . all of us the necessity of humility and meekness before the Lord, that He might teach us of His ways . . . [that we might] live by every word that proceedeth forth from His mouth" (*HC* 1:105).

"Freedom is based on truth, and no man is completely free as long as any part of his belief is based on error, for the chains of error bind his mind. This is why it is so important for us to learn all the truth we can . . . particularly . . . [from] the scriptures."

(N. Eldon Tanner, *Ensign,* May 1978, 14)

JULY 27
Nobility

Saturday, 27 Jul. 1844: John Taylor was with Joseph and Hyrum during the martyrdom and was critically wounded in the fray. John Taylor, who will later preside over the Church, now lies suffering from excruciating wounds. Poetess Eliza R. Snow contributes a sonnet entitled "To Elder John Taylor," which appears in the *Times & Seasons* and is this day entered into the official history of the Church. Here is an excerpt from the poetic tribute to his honor (see *HC* 7:211):

> *Thou Chieftain of Zion! henceforward thy name*
> *Will be classed with the martyrs and share in their fame;*
> *Through ages eternal, of thee will be said,*
> *"With the greatest of Prophets he suffered and bled."*

JULY 28
Trust in God

Thursday, 28 Jul. 1836: A letter from Daniel Dunklin, governor of Missouri, dated July 18, 1836, is received this day by the Saints in Liberty, Clay County, Missouri. The Saints, driven from Jackson County, had appealed to the governor for redress and for their protection from mob violence as they prepared to relocate in the northern part of the state. His reply is a classic of political buck-passing. For redress, he simply refers the Saints to the local courts; as for protection, he hides deftly behind public opinion. The Saints, he argues, need only prove their innocence (and thus shape public opinion) in order to be protected: "If you cannot do this, all I can say to you is that in this Republic the *vox populi* is the *vox Dei* [the voice of the people is the voice of God]" (*HC* 2:462). In a sweeping invocation of moral relativism, the governor leaves the Saints to their fate, showing once again that man can only trust in God for ultimate justice and salvation.

JULY 29
Leadership

Saturday, 29 Jul. 1843: At a meeting of the Quorum of the Twelve in Nauvoo, President Brigham Young gives instruction on the principles of presidency: "A man should, in the first place preside over himself, his passions, his person, and bring himself into subjection to the law of God; then preside over his children and his wife in righteousness; then he will be capable of presiding over a branch of the Church. . . . The first principle of our cause and work is to understand that there is a prophet in the Church, and that he is at the head of the Church of Jesus Christ on earth. . . . Inasmuch as he was called by God, and not the people, he is accountable to God only. . . . (*HC* 5:521–522).

"The Church will not dictate to any man, but it will counsel, it will persuade, it will urge, and it will expect loyalty from those who profess membership therein. . . . I make you a promise . . . that . . . I will never consent to nor advocate any policy, any program, any doctrine which will be otherwise than beneficial to the membership of this, the Lord's Church. This is His work. . . . He created its government."

(Gordon B. Hinckley, *Ensign,* May 2003, 60)

JULY 30
Build the Kingdom

Sunday, 30 Jul. 1837: George D. Watt becomes the first convert to be baptized in England, being baptized in the River Ribble near Preston, 30 miles north of Liverpool. He is accorded the honor of being the first of the nine converts to be baptized because he won a foot race to the river! (*CHFT*, 175). The work begins to flourish dramatically in Great Britain, many flocking to Zion over the next decade. By December 1847, there are 17,902 members in Great Britain, as compared with some 5,000 in the Salt Lake Valley (*HC* 7:629–630). From the abundance of Abrahamic descent in Great Britain comes great strength for the Church during its formative years.

"All Latter-day Saints enter the new and everlasting covenant when they enter this Church. They covenant to cease sustaining, upholding and cherishing the kingdom of the Devil. . . . They take a vow of the most solemn kind, before the heavens and earth, and that, too, upon the validity of their own salvation, that they will build up the Kingdom of God."

(Brigham Young, *Discourses of Brigham Young*, 160)

JULY 31

The Prophet As Deliverer

Tuesday, 31 Jul. 1838: When David W. Patten was ordained to the Apostleship in February 1835, he received a blessing in which he was promised that he would "have a knowledge of the things of the Kingdom, from the beginning, and be able to tear down priestcraft like a lion" (*HC* 2:190). Now Joseph Smith adds to his journal an enlightening article by Elder Patten from the *Elder's Journal,* which treats the subject of the scattering and gathering of Israel and the grafting in of the Gentiles into the natural roots. Taking Romans 11 as his text, Elder Patten provides a literal fulfillment of his blessing in testifying to the role which the Prophet Joseph Smith plays in the fulfillment of scriptural prophecy during the latter days as a "deliverer" of Israel (i.e., type of the Savior) under the inspiration of the Almighty (*HC* 3:49–54).

AUGUST

Nevertheless, Zion shall escape if she observe to do all things whatsoever I have commanded her.

—D&C 97:25

AUGUST 1
Good Works

◆───❦✦❦───◆

Monday, 1 Aug. 1831: Many sections of the Doctrine & Covenants are so full of wisdom and comfort that they need little commentary. Section 58, received this day, is one such revelation. The Prophet and other groups had just arrived in Jackson County, and all were eager to learn the Lord's will for them in the new gathering place (*HC* 1:190–195). Here is a sampling of the wisdom of the Lord unto them on this day: "For behold, it is not meet that I should command in all things; for he that is compelled in all things, the same is a slothful and not a wise servant; wherefore he receiveth no reward. Verily I say, men should be anxiously engaged in a good cause, and do many things of their own free will, and bring to pass much righteousness; For the power is in them, wherein they are agents unto themselves. And inasmuch as men do good they shall in no wise lose their reward" (vv. 26–28).

AUGUST 2

Zion

Tuesday, 2 Aug. 1831: Under the direction of the Prophet Joseph Smith, the "land of Zion" (centered at Jackson County, Missouri; see *HC* 1:196) is consecrated and dedicated by Sidney Rigdon. At the same time, the foundation of Zion is laid, symbolically, in the form of a log carried and put in place by 12 brethren from the Colesville Branch, representing the 12 tribes of Israel. Exactly two years later to the day, the Lord gives instructions to His persecuted Saints in Missouri: "Verily I say unto you, all among them who know their hearts are honest, and are broken, and their spirits contrite, and are willing to observe their covenants by sacrifice—yea, every sacrifice which I, the Lord, shall command—they are accepted of me. For I, the Lord, will cause them to bring forth as a very fruitful tree which is planted in a goodly land, by a pure stream, that yieldeth much precious fruit" (D&C 97:8–9).

AUGUST 3
Temple at Independence

Wednesday, 3 Aug. 1831: Prophecies detail two great temples to be built in the last days, which must be completed prior to Christ's Second Advent: the first in Jerusalem, the ancient Zion, and the second in the New Jerusalem, the New Zion. Faith is required to foresee the construction of either temple. On this day, Joseph Smith, together with other Church leaders, dedicates the spot for the great latter-day temple in Independence, Missouri. The service begins with the reading of the 87th Psalm, which portends the majesty of a perfected Zion. A single stone is then laid in place marking the Southeast corner of the temple's foundation (see *CHFT*, 107).

"The fact remains that the City Zion, or New Jerusalem, will eventually be built in Jackson County, Missouri, and the temple of the Lord will also be constructed. . . . [We] may be assured . . . the way shall be opened for the accomplishment . . . [of this purpose], and all opposition will melt like the hoar frost before the rising sun."

(Joseph Fielding Smith, *Improvement Era*, 33:469)

AUGUST 4
Out of Small Things

Thursday, 4 Aug. 1831: The first conference of the Church is held in "Zion" (Missouri) at the home of Joshua Lewis, in Kaw Township, some 12 miles west of Independence (see *HC* 1:199). In another spiritual event, exactly six years later to the day, the first confirmation of a convert in England is pronounced by Heber C. Kimball upon the head of 19-year-old Jennetta Richards, daughter of a local minister in Preston, near Liverpool (see *HC* 2:504–505). In a fascinating turn of events, Elder Kimball casually mentioned such in a letter to Willard Richards: "Willard, I baptized your wife today." The prophecy was fulfilled when Willard and Jennetta wed the following year (see Leon R. Hartshorn, *Exceptional Stories from the Lives of Our Apostles,* 122–124). What small acts of righteousness today will yield great blessings for you and your loved ones tomorrow?

AUGUST 5
Succession of the Presidency

Monday, 5 Aug. 1844: Sidney Rigdon, claimed during Sunday services the previous day that he should be named guardian of the Church in Joseph's place (*HC* 7:224). On this day, he meets in council with five of the Twelve to declare as much. Elder Rigdon then calls for a general meeting to ask the Saints who should direct the affairs of the kingdom. Brigham Young and others of the Twelve arrive in Nauvoo from their missions just in time to attend the meeting and spoil Rigdon's strategy to usurp authority. During the meeting, held on August 8, 1844, Brigham Young is miraculously transformed into the image, person, and voice of Joseph Smith in the perception of many observers (*HC* 7:236). The mantle of Church leadership falls upon Brigham Young as the President of the Twelve.

"The keys, though vested in all of the Twelve, are used by any one of them to a limited degree only, unless and until one of them attains that seniority which makes him the Lord's anointed on earth."

(Bruce R. McConkie, *Ensign,* May 1983, 22–23)

AUGUST 6
Settlement of the Salt Lake Valley

Saturday, 6 Aug. 1842: While attending to some business in Montrose, Iowa, the Prophet engages in relaxing conversation with some of his colleagues as they drink ice water in the shade of a schoolhouse. His tumbler in hand, the Prophet gives voice to visionary inspiration, prophesying, before he dies, that the true Church would be preserved in the West, and from there go to the world.

"I prophesied that the Saints would continue to suffer much affliction and would be driven to the Rocky Mountains, many would apostatize, others would be put to death by our persecutors or lose their lives in consequence of exposure or disease, and some of you will live to go and assist in making settlements and build cities and see the Saints become a mighty people in the midst of the Rocky Mountains."

(Joseph Smith, *HC* 5:85)

AUGUST 7
An Eye Single to God

Saturday, 7 Aug. 1831: Joseph Smith relates: "I attended the funeral of Sister Polly Knight, wife of Joseph Knight, Sen. This was the first death in the Church in this land, [Zion], and I can say, a worthy member sleeps in Jesus till the resurrection" (*HC* 1:199). The Knight family was loyal to Joseph and his cause even prior to his receiving the gold plates. On the family's journey to Missouri from Kirtland, Polly Knight's health worsened. "Yet," relates her son Newel, "she would not consent to stop traveling; her only . . . desire was to set her feet upon the land of Zion, and to have her body interred in that land" (*HC* 1:199).

"Generally speaking, 'an eye single to the glory of God' means sacrifice. It means that instead of endlessly doing what we want to do, we have to do what the Lord wants us to do."

(Hartman Rector Jr., *Ensign,* Dec. 1971, 64)

AUGUST 8
Declare Repentance

Monday, 8 Aug. 1831: Following a special conference in Kirtland on June 3–6, 1831, 28 elders are called on a mission to Missouri for a conference to be held there two months hence, preaching the gospel on the way (see D&C 52; *HC* 1:175–179). Now, the Missouri conference having ended, the Prophet receives Section 60 concerning that mission. In general, the Lord is pleased. "But with some I am not well pleased, for they will not open their mouths, but they hide the talent which I have given unto them, because of the fear of man. Wo unto such, for mine anger is kindled against them. And it shall come to pass, if they are not more faithful unto me, it shall be taken away, even that which they have" (vv. 2–3) Do you suppose those so addressed in this "interim report card" did a better job on the return journey?

"It has been a time of warning from the day when the Prophet first received the manifestation from the heavens that the gospel was to be restored. . . . Our mission in all the world, and also in the stakes of Zion is, Repent ye, for the kingdom of heaven is at hand."

(Joseph Fielding Smith, CR, Oct. 1919, 88)

AUGUST 9

Looking Out for Others

Tuesday, 9 Aug. 1831: Having filled their church assignments in Missouri, Joseph Smith and his companions start for Kirtland by canoeing down-river. The Prophet recalls: "Nothing very important occurred till the third day, when many of the dangers so common upon the western waters manifested themselves; and after we had encamped upon the bank of the river, at McIlwaine's Bend, Brother Phelps, in open vision by daylight, saw the destroyer in his most horrible power ride upon the face of the waters; others heard the noise, but saw not the vision" (*HC* 2:202–203). Three days later the Prophet receives Section 61, wherein the Lord rebukes the elders for traveling swiftly past towns on either bank where people are "perishing in unbelief," uncon-cerned about the true peril—spiritual death (v. 3).

AUGUST 10
The Sacrament

❧❧❧❧❧

Wednesday, 10 Aug. 1830: Some time in early August, the Prophet is visited at his home in Harmony, Pennsylvania, by Newel Knight and Sister Knight. ". . . and as neither his wife nor mine had been as yet confirmed, it was proposed that we should confirm them, and partake together of the Sacrament, before he and his wife should leave us. In order to prepare for this I set out to procure some wine for the occasion, but had gone only a short distance when I was met by a heavenly messenger, and received the following revelation" (then follows Section 27; see *HC* 1:106–108). The Lord makes clear concerning the emblems of the sacrament: "That it mattereth not what ye shall eat or what ye shall drink when ye partake of the sacrament, if it so be that ye do it with an eye single to my glory" (D&C 27:2).

"Do you remember the feeling you had when you were baptized—that sweet, clean feeling of a pure soul, having been forgiven, washed clean through the merits of the Savior? If we partake of the sacrament worthily, we can feel that way regularly, for we renew that covenant, which includes his forgiveness."

(John H. Groberg, *Ensign,* May 1989, 38)

AUGUST 11
Preparation

Friday, 11 Aug. 1843: An obituary notice appears in the *Times & Seasons* for General James Adams of Springfield. This close personal friend of the Prophet died of cholera. Two months later, during the final day of October conference, October 9, 1843, Joseph will deliver an inspired eschatological discourse—one having to do with the final or ultimate aspects of existence—which the Prophet says "is a subject we ought to study more than any other" (*HC* 6:50). Speaking of those beyond the veil, Joseph says "Spirits can only be revealed in flaming fire or glory. Angels have advanced further, their light and glory being tabernacled; and hence they appear in bodily shape. . . . Patriarch Adams is now one of the spirits of the just men made perfect; and, if revealed now, must be revealed in fire. . . . The spirits of the just are exalted to a greater and more glorious work and know and understand our thoughts, feelings, and motions" (*HC* 6:51–52). How carefully we should make our preparations for final things.

AUGUST 12
The Remnants

Thursday, 12 Aug. 1841: Approximately 100 American Indians visit the Prophet Joseph Smith in Nauvoo. He addresses them through an interpreter about "many things which the Lord had revealed unto me concerning their fathers, and the promises that were made concerning them in the Book of Mormon" (*HC* 4:401). For remarkable dialogue with several Pottawattamie chiefs on July 2, 1843, see *HC* 5:479–481. One of the chiefs said, "We have asked the Great Spirit to save us and let us live; and the Great Spirit has told us that he had raised up a great Prophet, chief, and friend, who would do us great good and tell us what to do; and the Great Spirit has told us that you are the man (pointing to the Prophet Joseph Smith)" (E. Cecil McGavin, *Nauvoo the Beautiful*, 80).

"President Taylor prayed: . . . 'Remember, O Lord, in mercy the Lamanites . . . to whose fathers thou promised that thou wouldest renew thy covenants to their seed. We thank thee that thou hast commenced to give unto them dreams and visions and they have begun to feel after thee.'"

(Howard W. Hunter, *Ensign,* Nov. 1975, 94)

AUGUST 13
Gratitude

Saturday, 13 Aug. 1831: On their return trip from Missouri to Kirtland, Joseph Smith and his companions have a pleasant chance encounter with several Elders on their way to Zion, and greet them with "joyful salutations" (*HC* 1:205). Joseph then receives Section 62. The brethren are assured that testimonies borne on earth are recorded in heaven (v. 3) and reminded of the necessity of having "a thankful heart" for all blessings. Six days before, Section 59 was given, which admonished: "And in nothing doth man offend God, or against none is his wrath kindled, save those who confess not his hand in all things, and obey not his commandments" (v. 21). Do we simply take the blessings in our lives for granted? Let us remember the instruction from the Apostle Paul: "In every thing give thanks: for this is the will of God in Christ Jesus concerning you" (2 Thess. 5:18).

AUGUST 14
Cheerfulness

Sunday, 14 Aug. 1842: "Spent the forenoon chiefly in conversation with Emma on various subjects, and in reading my history with her—both felt in good spirits and very cheerful" (*HC* 5:92). This is how the Prophet characterizes the pleasant morning he spends with this wife. (It is instructive that he reads "with her" and not "to her.") Their history is hardly filled with cheerful things: it is decidedly a mixture of triumphs and disappointments, advances and regressions, the sublime and the tragic. But, as seen above, the perspective of the Prophet and his wife is overwhelmingly positive, and they jointly celebrate the gracious hand of the Lord in bringing forth the gospel.

"Those who accept and live the teachings of our Savior find the strength to be of good cheer, for he declared, 'Whosoever will save his life shall lose it: and whosoever will lose his life for my sake shall find it' (Matt. 16:25). When we apply this principle in our lives and share it with our associates, it is possible to supplant discouragement, tragedy, and gloom with hope and cheer. The fruits of cheerfulness lie within each of us, side by side with our resolution, priorities, and desires."

(Marvin J. Ashton, *Ensign,* May 1986, 66)

AUGUST 15
Calm Leadership

Monday, 15 Aug. 1842: In May, a would-be assassin wounded ex-governor Lilburn W. Boggs in Missouri. Joseph Smith is accused of complicity in the crime—forcing him to hide on a Mississippi River island in order to elude his enemies. Rumors begin to multiply in Nauvoo regarding possible attacks from the militia, writs, etc., so that when some of the brethren (including his brother Hyrum) hasten to the Prophet this day to warn him of all sorts of real or imagined dangers, they have worked themselves into somewhat of a frenzy. Joseph calmly evaluates the situation: "I took occasion to gently reprove all present for letting report excite them, and advised them not to suffer themselves to be wrought upon by any report, but to maintain an even, undaunted mind. Each one began to gather courage, and all fears were soon subsided, and the greatest union and good feeling prevailed amongst all present" (*HC* 5:97–98). By this we see the wisdom of cultivating composure under stress, of carefully separating fact from fiction when making judgments, and, above all, of continually maintaining faith in the guidance of the Lord.

AUGUST 16
The Twelve

Monday, 16 Aug. 1841: A special conference of the Church is held at Nauvoo involving the Twelve Apostles. The day previous, the Prophet's infant son, Don Carlos, had passed away, so all members of the Twelve present visited the Prophet and Emma to console them. At the meeting, the Prophet introduces an important clarification of policy. While the Twelve to that point had been involved personally, for the most part, with missionary work away from the center of the Church and overseas, the time had now come "when the Twelve should be called upon to stand in their place next to the first Presidency" (*HC* 4:403). Thus the Twelve emerge in the stature proclaimed by the Lord: "A quorum, equal in authority and power to the three presidents [First Presidency]" (D&C 107:24). This important precedent ensured proper succession when, less than three years later, the Prophet was martyred.

AUGUST 17
Law and Order

Thursday, 17 Aug. 1835: A general assembly of the Church convenes in Kirtland to formally adopt the revelations collected for publication in the first edition of the Doctrine & Covenants. During the meeting, an article prepared by Oliver Cowdery on government and law is read and approved unanimously for inclusion (*HC* 2:247). It now comprises Section 134. The leaders of the Church were going on record—to refute public accusation—as unequivocally upholding constitutional principles. In the original version, the article's preamble reads: "That our belief with regard to earthly governments and laws in general may not be misinterpreted nor misunderstood, we have thought proper to present, at the close of this volume, our opinion concerning the same" (*HC* 2:247).

"To accuse us of being unfriendly to the Government, is to accuse us of hostility to our religion, for no item of inspiration is held more sacred with us than the Constitution under which she acts."

(Brigham Young, *Discourses of Brigham Young*, 359)

AUGUST 18
Faith

Saturday, 18 Aug. 1832: This month, the Prophet Joseph Smith receives the word of the Lord to John Murdock (Section 99), calling him to serve as a missionary in the eastern states. In 1831, Brother Murdock's wife had passed away while giving birth to twins—on the very same day Emma Smith had lost her twins when they were but a few hours old. Knowing of Emma's heartache, and having no wife to care for his newborn son and daughter, Brother Murdock gave them to Joseph and Emma to raise (*HC* 1:260). Steadfast faith in the Lord despite trials is demonstrated by this brother time after time. Despite the sacrifice of giving his children to the Prophet, he was one of the faithful early converts to the Church and was to participate in Zion's Camp and serve as a bishop, high counselor, and (in Utah) as patriarch.

AUGUST 19

Sacrifice

Tuesday, 19 Aug. 1834: This is a good day to recall the exemplary devotion of the faithful women who helped with the construction of the Lord's temple in Kirtland. Heber C. Kimball reported concerning the summer of 1834: "Our women were engaged in knitting and spinning, in order to clothe those who were laboring at the building; and the Lord only knows the scenes of poverty, tribulation and distress which we passed through to accomplish it. My wife had toiled all summer in lending her aid towards its accomplishment. She took a hundred pounds of wool to spin on shares, which, with the assistance of a girl, she spun, in order to furnish clothing for those engaged in building the temple . . ." (Orson F. Whitney, *Life of Heber C. Kimball,* 68).

". . . I say that those women have borne the heat and burden of those early and trying days and God will bless them for evermore. And besides all this, they have stepped forward and done the works of Sarah . . . . I feel to bless all such . . ."

(Heber C. Kimball, *Journal of Discourses,* 10:166)

AUGUST 20
Prophets

Saturday, 20 Aug. 1842: In a meeting near the temple site in Nauvoo, Sidney Rigdon relates a miraculous experience concerning his daughter, Eliza. The ailing girl had been declared dead by her attending physician. However, she returned to deliver prophetic messages concerning her family and others, and to explain she was sent back "because that her father had dedicated her to God, and prayed to Him for her, that he would restore her back to him again" (*HC* 5:122). Rigdon bears testimony of his convictions about the restored gospel and Joseph's role as Prophet. Yet he was excommunicated on September 8, 1844 for refusal to accede to the authority of the Twelve. About this same time, he prophesied that not one more stone would be laid on the rising walls of the Nauvoo Temple, whereupon a priesthood brother and two companions walked over and placed a stone, declaring Sidney a false prophet.

AUGUST 21
Health

Thursday, 21 Aug. 1834: During this era some areas of the United States were experiencing a mortality rate among infants as high as 60 percent within the first year of life. In addition, a cholera epidemic had been sweeping the eastern states as well as around the world—killing thousands in its wake (see *HC* 1:282). Dr. Frederick G. Williams, counselor in the First Presidency, is dispatched this day from Kirtland on a medical mission to nearby Cleveland to "commence administering to the sick, for the purpose of obtaining blessings for them, and for the glory of the Lord" (*HC* 2:146). Lyman Wight is also charged with teaching false doctrine that "all disease in this Church is of the devil, and that medicine administered to the sick is of the devil; for the sick in the Church ought to live by faith" (*HC* 2:147). President Joseph Smith corrects Elder Wight on both accounts, implying that disease is often simply a weakness of the flesh common to all men, and stating that God blesses mankind with unique herbs and other remedies for the benefit of His children, which are to be used with "prudence and thanksgiving" (*Word of Wisdom*).

AUGUST 22
Friendship

Monday, 22 Aug. 1842: The Prophet Joseph Smith spends much of the month in secret seclusion away from Nauvoo, at the home of a trusted associate, Edward Sayers (*HC* 5:90). The Prophet's dramatic escape, clandestine meetings, and danger-filled exile cause him to reflect once again how grateful he is, while among ruthless enemies, to have the unflinching support of so many dear friends. Concerning Emma: "Tongue cannot express the gratitude of my heart, for the warm and true-hearted friendship you have manifested in these things towards me" (*HC* 5:103). Concerning those who rowed him to safety in a skiff: "My heart would have been harder than an adamantine stone, if I had not prayed for them with anxious and fervent desire. I did so, and the still small voice whispered to my soul: These, that share your toils with such faithful hearts, shall reign with you in the kingdom of their God" (*HC* 5:109).

AUGUST 23
Judgment

Saturday, 23 Aug. 1834: Following Zion's Camp, Sylvester Smith berates Joseph Smith, accusing the Prophet of unchristian-like conduct while on their march to Missouri. From the testimony of several witnesses given this day at a special conference at Kirtland, quite the opposite appears to be the case: Sylvester Smith's character is brought into question, while that of Brother Joseph is exonerated. The findings of the hearing state, in part: "We have investigated [the Prophet's] whole proceedings by calling upon those who accompanied him to and from Missouri, and we are . . . satisfied . . . that he has acted in every respect worthy [of] his high and responsible station in this Church, and that those reports could have originated in the minds of none except . . . as . . . misunderstanding, or a natural jealousy" (*HC* 2:148).

"We should refrain from anything that seems to be a final judgment of any person . . . the Lord alone has the capacity to judge. . . . And, in all of this we must remember the command to forgive."

(Dallin H. Oaks, *Ensign*, Aug. 1999, 13)

AUGUST 24

Zion

Wednesday, 24 Aug. 1831: Late in August 1831, the Lord reveals important principles upon which the gathering to Zion is to be accomplished (Section 63). The previous month, He had identified Independence, Missouri, as the center place for Zion (D&C 57:1–3), and the Saints were anxious to know how to proceed. The Lord identifies key qualities of a Zion people: (1) they don't seek signs (see v. 9), (2) they are pure (see v. 16), (3) they are obedient (see v. 23), (4) they are astute, purchasing property by lawful means and moving circumspectly (see v. 29), and (5) they are generous (see v. 48). Two additional key qualities of a Zion people are humility (v. 57) and reverence in using the Lord's name (v. 64).

"Zion can be built up only among those who are the pure in heart . . . . Zion is to be in the world and not of the world, not dulled by a sense of carnal security, nor paralyzed by materialism. . . . Zion is 'every man seeking the interest of his neighbor and doing all things with an eye single to the glory of God' (D&C 82:19)."

(Spencer W. Kimball, *Ensign,* Mar. 1985, 4)

AUGUST 25
Faithful Service

Wednesday, 25 Aug. 1841: Oliver Granger, a great man and dear friend to the Prophet Joseph, dies at Kirtland at age 47 (*HC* 4:408–409). When Joseph Smith was forced to flee Kirtland for his life in January 1838, many accused him of "running away, cheating [his] creditors, etc." (*HC* 3:164). He had been under necessity of hiring Granger to close his affairs in the East. Elder Granger was in a sense thrown back into a hornet's nest among enemies of the Prophet and the Church in an attempt to satisfy debts and pacify contrary public opinion, and yet, though nearly totally blind, he performed his assignment so effectively that one of the creditors later writes that his management "has been truly praiseworthy, and has entitled him to my highest esteem, and ever grateful recollection" (*HC* 3:174).

"To each of us the Lord has said, 'Magnify your calling.' It is not always easy. But it is always rewarding. It blesses him who holds this divine authority."

(Gordon B. Hinkley, *Ensign,* May 1989, 46)

AUGUST 26
Gathering

Thursday, 26 Aug. 1841: A few days after the Prophet had announced that the Twelve were to shift their focus from traveling abroad to building up the stakes of Zion at home, the Apostles issue an important epistle to the Church, calling them together to Nauvoo, "where they will have the privilege of instruction from the First Presidency, and thereby understanding principle and doctrine, not to be learned elsewhere. . . . This is the place where the Elders are to receive instruction concerning their ministry, so as to become successful ministers of the dispensation of the fulness of times . . . prepared for the reception of the Lord Jesus" (*HC* 4:409–410). In our day we have the privilege of gathering to Zion wherever her stakes are established, and of being instructed directly from the prophet and other General Authorities via modern telecommunications.

AUGUST 27
Happiness

Saturday, 27 Aug. 1842: Joseph Smith addresses the subject of exhaltation in a remarkable essay he pens this day, which begins: "Happiness is the object and design of our existence; and will be the end thereof, if we pursue the path that leads to it; and this path is virtue, uprightness, faithfulness, holiness, and keeping all the commandments of God" (*HC* 5:134–135). In the final analysis, the Prophet writes the Lord's words: "For I delight in those who seek diligently to know my precepts, and abide by the law of my kingdom; for all things shall be made known unto them in mine own due time, and in the end they shall have joy" (*HC* 5:136).

"I plead with each of you to remember that wickedness never was happiness and that sin leads to misery. . . . We cannot achieve lasting happiness by pursuing the wrong things."

(Dallin H. Oaks, *Ensign,* Nov. 1991, 74–75)

AUGUST 28
Submissiveness

Thursday, 28 Aug. 1834: The High Council at Kirtland tries the case against Sylvester Smith, accused of violating the laws of the Church by slandering the character of the Prophet Joseph Smith (see *HC* 2:150–160). Sylvester Smith (no relation to the Prophet) had displayed a rebellious spirit during the march of Zion's Camp, and had rejected the Prophet's correction and counsel. One example cited at the trial is his refusal to share his bread with Parley P. Pratt one evening, when the latter had none, and his subsequent rejection of the Prophet's rebuke for the same (*HC* 2:157). After two days of trial, the council exacts from Sylvester Smith a written confession of error. To his credit, the latter then publishes in the *Messenger and Advocate* a contrite apology and testimony: "I admitted thoughts into my heart which were not right concerning him [the Prophet] . . ." (*HC* 2:160).

"When a man is capable of correcting you, and of giving you light, and true doctrine, do not get up an altercation but submit to be taught like little children, and strive with all your might to understand."

(Brigham Young, *Discourses of Brigham Young*, 245)

AUGUST 29
Tolerance

Monday, 29 Aug. 1836: Joseph and Hyrum Smith, Sidney Rigdon, and Oliver Cowdery spent much of August 1836 in Massachusetts on a special mission, and during their sojourn in Boston the Prophet reminisced on the subject of religious intolerance: "The early settlers of Boston (the Emporium of New England), who had fled from their mother country to avoid persecution and death, soon became so lost to principles of justice and religious liberty as to whip and hang the Baptist and the Quaker, who like themselves, had fled tyranny to a land of freedom; and the fathers of Salem from 1692 to 1693, whipped, imprisoned, tortured, and hung many of their citizens for supposed witchcraft. . . . Well did the Savior say concerning such, 'by their fruits you shall know them'" (*HC* 2:464–465). Ironically, intolerance has at times crept into the hearts of some of the Saints, contrary to all reason and revelation.

AUGUST 30
Sharing the Gospel

Sunday, 30 Aug. 1840: Because they are refused a forum in the local churches in London, despite ten days of campaigning, missionaries Heber C. Kimball, Wilford Woodruff, and George A. Smith preach in the open air at street meetings. When the police turn them away at Smithfield Market, they follow a local watchmaker, Henry Connor, to nearby Tabernacle Square. Here they are able to preach their sermons, despite some opposition from local leaders: "The people gave good attention, and seemed much interested in what they had heard. The inhabitants who lived around the square opened their windows to four stories high; the most of them were crowded with anxious listeners, which is an uncommon occurrence. The meeting was dismissed in the midst of good feeling" (*HC* 4:184). As a result of this and later meetings, Mr. Connor requested baptism.

AUGUST 31
Speaking Evil

⟡

Wednesday, 31 Aug. 1842: The Prophet Joseph Smith addresses the Female Relief Society and counsels them regarding opposition: "When wicked and corrupt men oppose, it is a criterion to judge if a man is warring the Christian warfare. When all men speak evil of you falsely, blessed are ye, etc. Shall a man be considered bad, when men speak evil of him? No. If a man stands and opposes the world of sin, he may expect to have all wicked and corrupt spirits arrayed against him. But it will be but a little season, and all these afflictions will be turned away from us, inasmuch as we are faithful, and are not overcome of these evils" (*HC* 5:140–141). To insure we don't become part of the problem, the Prophet urges: "If you have evil feelings, and speak of them to one another, it has a tendency to do mischief. . . . I now counsel you, that if you know anything calculated to disturb the peace or injure the feelings of your brother or sister, hold your tongues, and the least harm will be done" (*HC* 5:141).

SEPTEMBER

*The gospel [shall] roll forth . . . as the stone
which is cut out of the mountain without
hands . . . [filling] the whole earth.*

—D&C 65:2

SEPTEMBER 1
Tribulation

Thursday, 1 Sept. 1842: While in hiding to preserve his life from the onslaughts of persecutors, Joseph Smith writes an inspired letter to the Saints giving instruction on baptism for the dead and the importance of keeping proper records and using witnesses. The letter is canonized and becomes Section 127 (see *HC* 5:142–144). The Prophet writes of the persecutions he has endured: "And as for the perils which I am called to pass through, they seem but a small thing to me, as the envy and wrath of man have been my common lot all the days of my life . . . deep water is what I am wont to swim in. It all has become a second nature to me; and I feel, like Paul, to glory in tribulation" (v. 2). The honorable and the faithful will rise above tribulation and account it a privilege to contribute their part to the building up of the kingdom of God.

SEPTEMBER 2
Lamanites

Thursday, 2 Sept. 1830: September–October 1830 marks the beginning of missionary work among the Lamanites. Section 28 is given on behalf of Oliver Cowdery during the month of September: "[You] shall go unto the Lamanites and preach my gospel unto them; and inasmuch as they receive thy teachings thou shalt cause my church to be established among them" (v. 8). This moment had been anticipated by the Lord from the beginning, and the outcome was clear: "But before the great day of the Lord shall come, Jacob shall flourish in the wilderness, and the Lamanites shall blossom as the rose" (D&C 49:24).

"In a proclamation of the Twelve Apostles . . . in 1845, we are told—speaking of the Lamanites of North and South America—'They will also come to the knowledge of their forefathers, and of the fullness of the gospel; and they will embrace it and become a righteous branch of the house of Israel.' . . . Brigham Young . . . [said of them]: 'Look to see them like a flame of fire, a mighty rushing torrent, like the grand march of angels.'"

(J. Thomas Fyans, *Ensign,* May 1976, 12)

SEPTEMBER 3
Consecration

Saturday, 3 Sept. 1842: Joseph Smith makes the following journal entry this day: "In the morning at home, in company with John R. Boynton" (*HC* 5:144). John Boynton had previously been an Apostle in the Quorum of the Twelve (see *HC* 2:187, 191), but apostatized during the turbulent Kirtland period in 1837. The reunion of Prophet and apostate seems rather unusual, but certainly not out of character for the always-forgiving Joseph. One can only wonder what might have become of the gifted Dr. Boynton had he remained faithful to the Church and exercised his God-given talents in the service of the Lord. As it stands, after he left the Church he became a moderately accomplished scientist and an inventor of some renown, credited with inventing the portable chemical fire extinguisher, the soda fountain, and numerous other modern conveniences. He was recognized as an able physician, gold-mine engineer, published writer, genealogist, and geologist—trading celestial glory for the world's glory.

SEPTEMBER 4
Obedience

Wednesday, 4 Sept. 1833: On this day Joseph Smith pens a letter to Sister Vienna Jacques, who had moved to Missouri by divine command (see D&C 90:28–31), assuring her that the Lord was mindful of her sacrifice: "Let your heart be comforted; live in strict obedience to the commandments of God, and walk humbly before Him, and He will exalt thee in His own due time. I will assure you that the Lord has respect unto the offering you made" (*HC* 1:408). The only LDS woman besides Emma Smith to be mentioned in the Doctrine & Covenants, Vienna had left her nursing trade in Boston to join the Saints in Kirtland, where she was baptized and willingly consecrated all her savings of some $1,400 to the Church (see Susan Easton Black, *Who's Who in the Doctrine & Covenants*, 145).

SEPTEMBER 5
Unrighteous Dominion

Monday, 5 Sept. 1842: Joseph Smith copies into his journal a touching letter written by the Female Relief Society to Governor Thomas Carlin of Illinois, pleading that he not succumb to pressures to extradite their Prophet back to trial and certain assassination. "Your Excellency will bear with us if we remind you of the cold-blooded atrocities that we witnessed in that state [Missouri]. Our bosoms heave with horror, our eyes are dim, our knees tremble, our hearts are faint, when we think of their horrid deeds; and if the petitions of our husbands, brothers, fathers, and sons will not answer with your Excellency, we beseech you to remember that of their wives, mothers, sisters, and daughters" (*HC* 5:147). In response to a similar petition that Emma Smith had sent him a few days earlier, on August 27, Carlin writes a great deal of rhetoric under the color of law, but essentially ignores the pleas of desperation, thereby exercising unrighteous dominion by trampling upon his oath of office to honor the Constitution and protect the rights of all citizens (see *HC* 5:153–155).

SEPTEMBER 6

Joy

Tuesday, 6 Sept. 1842: The Prophet Joseph Smith writes an important letter to the Church concerning the doctrine and practice of baptism for the dead (later incorporated as Section 128; see *HC* 5:148–153). The theme is the availability of universal salvation, with the power to embrace all those who die without a knowledge of the gospel: "[They] without us cannot be made perfect—neither can we without our dead be made perfect" (v. 15, referring to Heb. 11:40). There is no place in scripture where the key elements of the restoration of all things in the dispensation of the fulness of times are more lyrically or joyfully summarized. "Let the mountains shout for joy, and all ye valleys cry aloud; and all ye seas and dry lands tell the wonders of your Eternal King! And ye rivers, and brooks, and rills, flow down with gladness. Let the woods and all the trees of the field praise the Lord; and ye solid rocks weep for joy! And let the sun, moon, and the morning stars sing together, and let all the sons of God shout for joy! And let the eternal creations declare his name forever and ever! . . ." (v. 23).

SEPTEMBER 7
Honoring Heritage

Friday, 7 Sept. 1838: On July 6, over 500 Saints known as the Kirtland Camp left Ohio to join their fellow Saints in Missouri. Little did they know the hardships awaiting them along the trail or the hornet's nest of mob activity they would encounter upon their arrival. Today, September 7, two months into their journey, camp historian Elias Smith records: "Sometime in the night a daughter of Otis Shumway died; and in the morning a child of J.A. Clark died" (*HC* 3:136). Milton V. Backman, Jr., reports: "Accidents and illness constantly afflicted the pioneers. Some persons were crushed under wagon wheels; others succumbed to disease. . . . They perspired by day and slept on cold and sometimes damp terrain by night. They forded streams, climbed up and down inclines, and followed rutted roads and trails, continually weakened by fatigue, a meager and changing diet, and polluted drinking water. In the midst of their suffering and afflictions, they turned to their Heavenly Father for help" (*CHFT*, 179).

"The foremost quality of our pioneers was *faith*"
(Dallin H. Oaks, *Ensign,* Nov. 1997, 72–74)

SEPTEMBER 8
Spiritual Gifts

Monday, 8 Sept. 1834: At a conference of elders in new Portage, Ohio, the Prophet Joseph Smith settles an interesting dispute and teaches a memorable lesson about the gift of tongues. One of the priesthood brethren had previously been tried before a Church council and given a period of time to reflect and repent. Another brother had then spoken in tongues, declaring that the defendant should be shown no leniency. Someone at this conference asked if that was correct procedure. "President Joseph Smith then gave an explanation of the gift of tongues, that it was particularly instituted for the preaching of the Gospel to other nations and languages, but it was not given for the government of the Church" (*HC* 2:162). Thus the use of tongues to provide testimony against another "was contrary to the rules and regulations of the Church, because in all our decisions we must judge from actual testimony" (*HC* 2:162). We are therefore reminded that gifts are given to us as a means to lift others up, to edify and not demean.

SEPTEMBER 9

Children

Friday, 9 Sept. 1842: For some time, the Prophet Joseph Smith had been away from his family and the Saints due to lawless Missouri ruffians who sought to put him on mock trial. This evening he is visited by his wife Emma and others for conversation and counsel. At about midnight, under cover of darkness, they leave Joseph's hiding place together. He writes: "I accompanied the brethren and Emma to my house, remaining there a few minutes to offer a blessing upon the heads of my sleeping children" (*HC* 5:160). The loving prophet-father risks his own safety for a moment with his beloved children.

"Next to eternal life, the most precious gift that our Father in heaven can bestow upon man is his children."

(David O. McKay, *Gospel Ideals,* 487)

SEPTEMBER 10
Water of Life

Monday, 10 Sept. 1832: The Prophet's cousin, George A. Smith, is baptized (*HC* 1:285). This stalwart man served in numerous Church functions throughout life. After his first mission, George suffered from rheumatic affliction. Joseph counseled: "You should never get discouraged, whatever your difficulties may be. If you are sunk in the lowest pit in Nova Scotia and all the Rocky Mountains piled on top of you, you ought not to be discouraged but to hang on, exercise faith and keep up good courage, and you will come out on top of the heap" (quoted in Susan Easton Black, *Who's Who in the Doctrine & Covenants*, 278). He was healed of his condition in a remarkable manner under the hands of the Prophet (*HC* 2:354). While with Zion's Camp in May 1834, George "discovered a spring that with a little digging furnished us with an abundant supply of excellent water" (*HC* 2:73). This meaning was not lost on all those who, like George, had drunk from the source of life (see Mo-iah 18:30).

SEPTEMBER 11
Forgiveness

Sunday, 11 Sept. 1831: The important and memorable revelation in Section 64 is received by the Prophet Joseph Smith. Upon his return from conducting Church business in Independence, he finds many of the Kirtland Saints disgruntled with each other—some have even apostatized—and few are paying their offerings to the Church. The answer to the problem is clear: The Saints are commanded to forgive one another, while the unrepentant are to be called to task before the Church. Disgruntled Saints in Kirtland (as in the Church today) are to repent, soften their hearts, and forgive one another, "that God may be glorified" (vv. 10, 12–13).

"Closely related to our own obligation to repent is the generosity of letting others do the same . . . In this we participate in the very essence of the Atonement of Jesus Christ. . . . We don't want God to remember our sins, so there is something fundamentally wrong in our relentlessly trying to remember [others' sins]. . . . It is one of those ironies of godhood that in order to find peace, the offended as well as the offender must engage the principle of forgiveness."

(Jeffery R. Holland, *Ensign,* Nov. 1996, 83)

SEPTEMBER 12
Conversion

Monday, 12 Sept. 1831: Close to this time, convert Ezra Booth, a former Methodist minister, announces his apostasy from the Church and begins to publish a series of virulent anti-Mormon letters. His conversion had come about when he had witnessed the Lord's miraculous healing of Mrs. Johnson under the hands of the Prophet (*HC* 1:215–216). However, his conversion was not anchored in spiritual conviction and, as the Prophet outlines in his journal, Booth was disappointed to learn that the gospel is founded on eternal principles: "That faith, humility, patience, and tribulation go before blessing, and that God brings low before He exalts" (*HC* 1:217). The Prophet compares Booth to those who flocked to the Savior after the miracle of the loaves and fishes, not out of spiritual hunger, but only because they were temporally filled. Booth has the dubious honor to be the first apostate of the Restoration to publish anti-Mormon literature, which (as the Prophet points out) "left him a monument of his own shame" (*HC* 1:217).

SEPTEMBER 13
Fruits of the Gospel

Wednesday, 13 Sept. 1843: A reprint of an article in *The New Haven Herald* appears in the *Nauvoo Neighbor,* entitled, "Nauvoo and Joseph Smith." It begins: "A gentleman . . . of undoubted veracity, who has lately spent several weeks at Nauvoo and among the Mormons, informs us that the general impression abroad in regard to that place and people is very erroneous. During his residence there he became quite familiar with their manners, principles, and habits, and says there is not a more industrious, moral, and well-ordered town in the country" (*HC* 6:32). We are reminded that the Saints have an obligation to bear the good fruits of gospel living. Is our crime rate significantly lower than the national pattern? Do we have a better record preserving our marriages? Are our educational achievements higher, and our charitable contributions more generous? Are we doing all we can—individually and collectively—to build up Zion?

SEPTEMBER 14
Devotion

Saturday, 14 Sept. 1839: Amid a severe malaria epidemic, Brigham Young leaves his home and sick family in Montrose, Iowa, for an apostolic mission to Great Britain. "His health was very poor; he was unable to go thirty rods to the river without assistance." (*HC* 4:9). On the 18th, the two Apostles, both still sick, leave the Kimball household in Nauvoo, that entire household also ailing. "'It seemed to me,' [Brother Kimball] later remarked, 'as though my very inmost parts would melt within me at the thought of leaving my family . . . almost in the arms of death. I felt as though I could scarcely endure it.' 'Hold up!' said he to the teamster, who had just started, 'Brother Brigham, this is pretty tough, but let us rise and give them a cheer.' Brigham, with much difficulty, rose to his feet, and joined Elder Kimball in swinging his hat and shouting, 'Hurrah, hurrah, hurrah, for Israel!'" Their wives, hearing the cheer, came to the door and "waved a farewell; and the two Apostles continued their journey, without purse, without scrip, for England" (*HC* 4:10).

SEPTEMBER 15
Fatherhood

Tuesday, 15 Sept. 1840: The funeral of Joseph Smith, Sr.—beloved Patriarch and father of the Prophet Joseph—takes place in Nauvoo. He died the previous day, at age 69, of consumption (tuberculosis) contracted during the expulsion of the Saints from Missouri. Of his father the Prophet remembers: "He was the first person who received my testimony after I had seen the angel, and exhorted me to be faithful and diligent to the message I had received. . . . He was one of the most benevolent of men; opening his house to all who were destitute. While at Quincy, Illinois, he fed hundreds of the poor saints who were flying from the Missouri persecutions, although he had arrived there penniless himself" (*HC* 4:190–191).

"The commandment to honor our parents echoes the sacred spirit of family relationships in which . . .we have sublime expressions of heavenly love . . . for one another. . . . We realize that our greatest expressions of joy or pain in mortality come from the members of our families."

(Dallin H. Oaks, *Ensign,* May 1991, 14)

SEPTEMBER 16
Revelation to the Church

Thursday, 16 Sept. 1830: Some days prior to the convening of the second conference of the Church on September 26, the Prophet Joseph Smith receives Sections 28 and 29, Section 28 stating that Joseph Smith "receive[s] commandments and revelations . . . even as Moses" (v. 2), and Section 29 being a call for the Saints to focus their hearts, minds, and energies on gathering the elect from among the peoples of the earth and preparing them for the coming day of judgment (see *HC* 1:111–115). The Lord lists the signs of the times to precede His return in glory. The millennial reign and ultimate celestialization of the earth are described. He explains that there is no special distinction between the types of commandments given to the children of men, since their origin is divine.

"We deal with many things which are thought to be not so spiritual; but all things are spiritual with the Lord, and he expects us to listen, and to obey, and to follow the commandments."

(Spencer W. Kimball, *Teachings of Spencer W. Kimball*, 376)

SEPTEMBER 17
Gathering

Sunday, 17 Sept. 1837: During a conference of priesthood leaders held at the Kirtland Temple, the Prophet Joseph Smith addresses them on the subject of the gathering of the Saints in the last days, and the duties of the different quorums in relation thereto (*HC* 2:513). He announces "that the places appointed for the gathering of the Saints were at this time crowded to overflowing, and that it was necessary that there be more stakes of Zion appointed in order that the poor might have a place to gather to" (*HC* 2:514). Concurrently, on September 18, 1837, the Presiding Bishopric sends a letter to the Saints abroad, asking them to consecrate their tithes and offerings for the support of the Lord's purposes: "Whatever pertains to salvation, either temporal or spiritual . . . all depend on our building up Zion according to the testimony of the Prophet" (*HC* 2:517).

"The gathering of Israel is both spiritual and temporal. The lost sheep gather spiritually when they join the Church, and they gather temporally when they come to a prepared place—that is, to Zion or one of her stakes."

(Bruce R. McConkie, *A New Witness for the Articles of Faith*, 569)

SEPTEMBER 18
Tithing

Monday, 18 Sept. 1837: Bearing this date, a letter from the Presiding Bishopric is sent throughout the Church asking the Saints to provide their tithes as a sacrifice for the building up of Zion. Following is a sample from this edifying missive: "It is the fixed purpose of our God, and has been so from the beginning . . . that the great work of the last days was to be accomplished by the tithing of His Saints" (*HC* 2:516). Furthermore it reads, "Let every Saint consider well the nature of his calling in the last days, and the great responsibility which rests upon him or her, as one to whom God has revealed His will; and make haste . . . to the building up of Zion. . . ." (*HC* 2:517). The gathering continues unabated today through the tithes, offerings, and sacrifices of the Saints.

"The law of tithing is a test by which the people as individuals shall be proved."

(Joseph F. Smith, *Gospel Doctrine: Selections from the Sermons and Writings of Joseph F. Smith,* 226)

SEPTEMBER 19

Pride

Saturday, 19 Sept. 1835: An unusual Church court is held to consider the case of Jared Carter, who is accused of pride and teaching false doctrine during a recent sermon. The final result is that he repents and seeks forgiveness, but we might benefit from avoiding the kinds of errors detailed in the minutes of the trial. Elder Hyrum Smith noted, "Pride had engendered in Elder Carter's heart a desire to excel, and the spirit of meekness was withdrawn, and he was left to err" (*HC* 2:279). This is a cogent reminder for us today to seek "a godly walk and conversation" (D&C 20:69).

"In the premortal council, it was pride that felled Lucifer, 'a son of the morning.' . . . The central feature of pride is enmity—enmity toward God and enmity toward our fellowmen. *Enmity* means 'hatred toward, hostility to, or a state of opposition.' . . . Pride is essentially competitive in nature. . . . Pride is a sin that can readily be seen in others but is rarely admitted in ourselves."

(Ezra Taft Benson, *Ensign,* May 1989, 4–5)

SEPTEMBER 20
Liberty

Wednesday, 20 Sept. 1843: The *Nauvoo Neighbor* carries an editorial on the exoneration of Orrin Porter Rockwell, one of Joseph Smith's bodyguards, accused of an assassination attempt on Lilburn W. Boggs, former governor of Missouri. As it turned out, the evidence did not support this accusation (made by the enemies of the Church). Rockwell is eventually freed, as the Prophet had prophesied (*HC* 5:305), and returns to Nauvoo on Christmas Day 1843, much to the Prophet's joy (*HC* 6:134)—but only after having to languish in jail for nearly ten months (compare Rockwell's account of his experiences in *HC* 6:135–142). The Prophet, who had been arrested as an accessory to the crime, was released when the Circuit Court of the United States for the District of Illinois determined that the charges lacked foundation (*HC* 5:231, 244). Once again, truth eventually prevails and becomes the vehicle for deliverance.

SEPTEMBER 21
Sealing Power

Sunday, 21 Sept. 1823: When 17 years old, Joseph Smith retires for the night in his family's log home at Manchester, New York. While yet in prayer he is visited by the angel Moroni, who informs Joseph that God had a work for him to do, and that his name "should be had for good and evil among all nations, kindreds, and tongues, or that it should be both good and evil spoken of among all people" (JS—H 1:33). Moroni repeats his visitation twice during the night, repeating prophecies about the future of the gospel and the sealing power that will bring the Lord's children to Him. After the third visit Joseph hears the cock crow, announcing a new day and the dawning of a new dispensation of the gospel.

"I thank him and love him [Joseph Smith] for the sealing power of the holy priesthood that makes possible . . . the continuance of the family through eternity. . . . If nothing else came out of all the . . . travail . . . of the Restoration than [this] . . . it would have been worth all that it has cost."

(Gordon B. Hinckley, *Teachings of Gordon B. Hinckley*, 475–476)

SEPTEMBER 22
Priesthood Covenants

Saturday, 22 Sept. 1832: On this day (and on the day following) one of the great revelations of the Restoration, concerning the oath and covenant of the priesthood, is given through the Prophet Joseph Smith (Section 84; see *HC* 1:286–295). Just five years previous, to the very day, the Prophet had been entrusted by the angel Moroni with the sacred plates containing a new witness for the Savior (*HC* 1:18). Now, with the translation and publication of the Book of Mormon complete, the Lord warns His people solemnly: "[Repent] and remember the new covenant, even the Book of Mormon and the former commandments which I have given them, not only to say, but to do according to that which I have written" (D&C 84:57). The Lord teaches His people how to enjoy the fulness of priesthood blessings, whereby each worthy priesthood holder and his family, in receiving and magnifying his calling, can merit this sublime reward: "[Therefore] all that my Father hath shall be given unto him" (v. 38).

SEPTEMBER 23

Honesty

Wednesday, 23 Sept. 1835: Joseph Smith records in his journal: "My heart is full of desire today, to be blessed of the God of Abraham with prosperity, until I shall be able to pay all my debts, for it is the delight of my soul to be honest" (*HC* 2:281). The Prophet equates the payment of debt with honesty. This is only one aspect of honesty, yet it is an important principle for our day and age, especially in light of easy consumer credit. In the event one becomes encumbered with debt, the Lord's policy is clear: "And again, verily I say unto you, concerning your debts—behold it is my will that you shall pay all your debts" (D&C 104:78).

"Our bankruptcy law is on the books for the rare occasion when true disaster strikes a family, and none of us would take away that protection. . . . There is a question asked of those who seek a temple recommend that deals with honesty. I sincerely hope that those who have taken unfair advantage of this just and proper law don't carry a temple recommend and feel that they're absolved from responsibilities."

(L. Aldin Porter, *Ensign*, Apr. 2002, 34)

SEPTEMBER 24
Wisdom of God

Friday, 24 Sept. 1830: About this time of the year in 1830, the Prophet Joseph Smith recommences the translation of the Book of Mormon after the loss of the initial 116 pages of the translation. In D&C chapter 10, the Lord warns the Prophet that Satan has put into the hearts of wicked men to induce him to retranslate the lost portion so that he might be caught in contradictions, they having altered the original version. So the Lord commands the Prophet to start again with a new source this time, i.e., the smaller plates of Nephi (see vv. 10–20, 41). Nearly a millennium and a half previous, the great prophet-abridger Mormon had prepared these smaller plates "for a wise purpose; for thus it whispereth me, according to the workings of the Spirit of the Lord which is in me," since "the Lord knoweth all things which are to come" (W of M 1:7). The Lord's wisdom is thus demonstrated to anticipate every possible need of His children (see D&C 3:1, 3).

"Every person on earth, in or out of the Church, can gain wisdom from the Lord, who is the source and font of all truth and righteousness."

(Bruce R. McConkie, *DNTC,* 3:245)

Saturday, 25 Sept. 1841: The Prophet records an interesting event in the life of Wilford Woodruff. After attending a conference on an island on Lake Michigan, Elder Woodruff and his family begin their return trip home to Nauvoo by boarding the steamer *Chesapeake.* Just before midnight "a tremendous storm of wind and rain" engulfs the craft (*HC* 4:418). Elder Woodruff recounts: "It blew a hurricane, and the lake became as rough as it could be by the force of wind. . . . We were some forty miles from land when the gale struck us, and I was awakened from a sound sleep by the cry, 'We are all lost.' The first thought that entered my mind was: 'No, we shall not be lost'" (*HC* 4:418). Likewise, we are often assaulted by storms from the adversary, and the only sure defense against such storms is to build upon the certain foundation of Christ.

Sunday, 26 Sept. 1830: The second conference of the Church takes place this month at Fayette, New York, during which time we had much of the power of God manifested amongst us; the Holy Ghost came upon us, and filled us with joy unspeakable; and peace, and faith, and hope, and charity abounded in our midst" (*HC* 1:115). Before the attendees depart, the Prophet Joseph Smith receives instruction for specific individuals (Sections 30 and 31), but which have relevance for all of us. David Whitmer is warned: "[You] have feared man and have not relied on me for strength as you ought . . ." (D&C 30:1–2). To Thomas Marsh: "Be patient in afflictions. . . . Govern your house in meekness, and be steadfast. . . . Pray always, lest you enter into temptation and lose your reward" (D&C 31:9, 12). Messages such as these—rely on God, follow the prophets, be humble and longsuffering, pray always, endure faithfully—are ever the substance of our prophets' teachings, then as today.

SEPTEMBER 27

Defense

Friday, 27 Sept. 1844: "This was the day set apart by the anti-Mormons for the great 'wolf hunt'" (*HC* 7:276). Governor Thomas Ford remembered this event in his *History of Illinois*: "In the course of the fall of 1844, the anti-Mormon leaders sent printed invitations to all the militia captains in Hancock, and to the captains of militia in all the neighboring counties of Illinois, Iowa, and Missouri, to be present with their companies at a great wolf hunt in Hancock; and it was privately announced that the wolves to be hunted were the Mormons and Jack-Mormons. Preparations were made for assembling several thousand men" (*HC* 7:45–46). At the time the usual anti-Mormon lies were printed in the newspapers to poison the public mind against the Saints. Governor Ford and about 500 troops march to the protection of Nauvoo, and the cowardly "wolf hunters" flee back into hiding (see *HC* 7:276–277).

SEPTEMBER 28
Sustaining Good Government

Saturday, 28 Sept. 1833: The Saints in Jackson County, Missouri, send a petition to Governor Daniel Dunklin, asking redress from the persecutions being heaped upon them. "Influenced by the precepts of our beloved Savior when we have been smitten on the one cheek, we have turned the other also; when we have been sued at the law, and our coat been taken, we have given them our cloak also; when they have compelled us to go with them a mile, we have gone with them twain; we have borne the above outrages without murmuring; but we cannot patiently bear them any longer; according to the laws of God and man, we have borne enough. Believing with all honorable men, that whenever that fatal hour shall arrive that the poorest citizen's person, property, or rights and privileges, shall be trampled upon by a lawless mob with impunity, that moment a dagger is plunged into the heart of the constitution, and the union must tremble!" (*HC* 1:414–415).

SEPTEMBER 29

Mortality

Sunday, 29 Sept. 1839: At a meeting in the log homestead of Joseph Smith at Nauvoo, a great principle is revealed by the Prophet. This dispels a common notion that when Saints are ill or become objects of misfortune, it is because they are unrighteous: "It is a false idea that the Saints will escape all the judgments, whilst the wicked suffer; for all flesh is subject to suffer, and 'the righteous shall hardly escape [see D&C 63:34];' still many of the Saints will escape, for the just shall live by faith; yet many of the righteous shall fall a prey to disease, to pestilence, etc., by reason of the weakness of the flesh, and yet be saved in the Kingdom of God. So that it is an unhallowed principle to say that such and such have transgressed because they have been preyed upon by disease or death, for all flesh is subject to death; and the Savior has said, 'Judge not, lest ye be judged'" (see *HC* 4:11).

SEPTEMBER 30
Companionship

Friday, 30 Sept. 1842: The Prophet spends the day with his wife, who had fallen ill the previous day. In fact, he stays with her for several more days, even though he himself is not well. In October, he writes: "My dear Emma was worse. Many fears were entertained that she would not recover. . . . She grew worse at night, and continued very sick indeed. I was unwell, and much troubled on account of Emma's sickness" (*HC* 5:167–168). Meanwhile, the Prophet has to carry out his official duties and contend with a variety of urgencies: certify the temple accounts, deal with the actions of apostates, learn that a reward had been placed on his head by the enemies of the Church, confront legal entanglements in Missouri, etc. Finally, on the 6th of October, Emma begins to recover. Joseph writes, "May the Lord speedily raise her to the bosom of her family, that the heart of His servant may be comforted again. Amen" (*HC* 5:168). By November 1 she is able to ride with her husband to the temple (*HC* 5:182).

OCTOBER

*My people, which are of the house of
Israel, shall be gathered home unto the
lands of their possessions . . .*

—NE. 29:14

OCTOBER 1
Self-Sufficiency

Tuesday, 1 Oct. 1844: The Twelve Apostles, acting under Quorum President Brigham Young, publish this day an "Epistle of the Twelve" to the Saints, giving a variety of instructions of both temporal and spiritual nature. Our priority is the gathering of the Saints, to be supported by the industry and united effort of the people. Modern prophets have repeatedly urged the Saints to become self-sufficient, and this epistle advocates that they manufacture their own products from raw materials rather than paying out diminishing cash reserves to outsiders for finished goods. In the epistle President Young exhorts: "Not only must farms be cultivated, houses built, and mills to grind the corn, but there must be something produced by industry, to send off to market in exchange for cash, and for such other articles we need" (*HC* 7:280–281).

"Nothing destroys the individuality of a . . . [person] as much as the failure to be self-reliant."

(Heber J. Grant, *Teachings of Presidents of the Church: Heber J. Grant,* 116)

OCTOBER 2
Home

Tuesday, 2 Oct. 1838: The Kirtland Camp of some 500 Saints arrives in Far West, Missouri, following a three-month, 870-mile trek from Kirtland, where mobs had displaced them from their homes. They were met by the First Presidency and escorted into the city. The next day they leave for Adam-ondi-Ahman, arriving at their destination at sunset on October 4th. One of the local brethren proclaims, "Brethren, your long and tedious journey is now ended; you are now on the public square of Adam-ondi-Ahman. This is the place where Adam blessed his posterity, when they rose up and called him Michael, the Prince, the Archangel, and he being full of the Holy Ghost predicted what should befall his posterity to the latest generation" (*HC* 3:148). But this haven was not to be their ultimate destination and many trials were endured and many waystations passed before the surviving Saints found relative peace in the tops of the Rocky Mountains.

OCTOBER 3
Banqueting with the Lord

Tuesday, 3 Oct. 1843. On this day around 100 couples assemble at the Nauvoo Mansion, home of the Prophet Joseph Smith and his family, to celebrate formally the opening of this comely building. From the *Nauvoo Neighbor* of this date: "General Joseph Smith, the proprietor of said house, provided a luxurious feast for a pleasure party . . ." (*HC* 6:42). Among the resolutions read is the following: "Nauvoo . . . the center of all centers . . . embracing the intelligence of all nations, with industry, frugality, economy, virtue, and brotherly love . . . [is] a suitable home for the Saints" (*HC* 6:42). The Saints celebrate their blessings and salute the Prophet as the head of their transitional home by enjoying a festive banquet symbolic, in a sense, of banqueting with the Lord.

"God's children . . . are . . . hungering and thirsting for pure Gospel truth, which they find not in man-made . . . philosophies; and blind leaders."

(Orson F. Whitney, CR, Oct. 1930, 47)

OCTOBER 4
Trust in God

Thursday, 4 Oct. 1838: A mob fires upon besieged Saints at DeWitt (northeast of Richmond and Independence, in Missouri), forcing the Saints to return fire in self-defense. The same day General Samuel D. Lucas writes to Governor Lilburn W. Boggs stating that because of such conflagrations "those base and degraded beings [the 'Mormons'] will be exterminated from the face of the earth" (*HC* 3:150). The Prophet Joseph Smith comments on the full letter: "Whoever heard before of high-minded and honorable men condescending to sacrifice their honor, by stooping to wage war, without cause or provocation, against 'base and degraded beings.' But General Lucas . . . knew the Saints were an innocent, unoffending people, and would not fight, only in self-defense" (*HC* 3:151).

"The knowledge that God is with us . . . should buoy us up under every . . . trial . . . .The very efforts of the enemies of His Church to hedge up its way will be overruled by Him to accelerate its advancement."

(Joseph F. Smith, John R. Winder, Anthon H. Lund, *Messages of the First Presidency,* 4:123)

OCTOBER 5
Priesthood

Monday, 5 Oct. 1840: On the last day of a three-day conference of the Church held at Nauvoo, a special article on the priesthood, written by the Prophet, is read to the congregation. This remarkable statement declares that the Melchizedek Priesthood "holds the highest authority which pertains to the Priesthood, and the keys of the Kingdom of God in all ages of the world to the latest posterity on the earth, and is the channel through which all knowledge, doctrine, the plan of salvation, and every important matter is revealed from heaven. . . . It is the channel through which the Almighty commenced revealing His glory at the beginning of the creation of this earth, and through which He has continued to reveal Himself to the children of men to the present time, and through which He will make known His purposes to the end of time" (*HC* 4:207).

"What a dark world this would be without priesthood blessings for you and me. . . . Through priesthood power we can receive the gift of the Holy Ghost to lead us to truth, testimony, and revelation."

(Robert D. Hales, *Ensign,* Nov. 1995, 32)

OCTOBER 6
Persistence

Saturday, 6 Oct. 1838: Joseph Smith arrives by stealth to aid the besieged community of DeWitt, Missouri, where the local Saints are surrounded by threatening mobs (*HC* 3:153). At the same time, in Far West, Missouri, Brigham Young and Thomas B. Marsh are presiding at a quarterly conference where John Taylor is sustained as an Apostle, and numerous missionaries are called to go forth to preach the gospel in the southern states. Even as the young Church is in desperate straits, beset by enemies on all sides, suffering degradations at the hands of mobs, and dealing with apostasy and slackening faith on the part of many, the work of the Lord goes forward unabated. Spiritual giants always step up to roll the work onward, no matter the obstacles.

"Let us alone, and we will send Elders to the uttermost parts of the earth, and gather our Israel, wherever they are; and if you persecute us, we will do it the quicker. . . . If you let us alone, we will do it a little more leisurely; but if you persecute us, we will sit up nights to preach the Gospel."

(Brigham Young, *Teachings of Presidents of the Church: Brigham Young,* 265)

OCTOBER 7

Bishops: Stewards of God

Wednesday, 7 Oct. 1835: Joseph Smith pronounces a beautiful blessing on behalf of Bishop Newel K. Whitney and prophesies that "the Bishopric shall never be taken away from him while he liveth. . . . He shall deal with a liberal hand to the poor and the needy, the sick and afflicted, the widow and the fatherless. And marvelously and miraculously shall the Lord his God provide for him, even that he shall be blessed with a fullness of the good things of this earth, and his seed after him from generation to generation. And it shall come to pass, that according to the measure that he meteth out with a liberal hand to the poor, so shall it be measured to him again by the hand of his God, even an hundred fold. Angels shall guard his house, and shall guard the lives of his posterity, and they shall become very great and very numerous on the earth" (*HC* 2:288).

"I cannot say enough in tribute to the great bishops of this Church, who serve without any compensation except the compensation that comes of the love of the people and the good commendation of the Lord whom they serve."

(Gordon B. Hinckley, *Ensign,* Jan. 1998, 73)

OCTOBER 8
Mothers in Israel

Wednesday, 8 Oct. 1845: Lucy Mack Smith, revered and aging mother of the Prophet Joseph, rises and speaks before some 5,000 Saints assembled for the last conference of the Church in Nauvoo. She exhorts all to protect their children from idleness by giving them work to do and books to read. She counsels all "to be full of love, goodness and kindness, and never to do in secret, what they would not do in the presence of millions" (*HC* 7:470–471). Then in a noble gesture, she wishes to learn whether the congregation might consider her a "mother in Israel," whereupon Brigham Young responds, "All who consider Mother Smith as a mother in Israel, signify it by saying yes!" According to the minutes, "One universal 'yes' rings throughout" (*HC* 7:471).

"As a rule the mothers . . . of Israel, are the very best women that live in the world . . . . The good influence that a good mother exercises over her children is like leaven cast into the measure of meal, that will leaven the whole lump; and as far as her influence extends."

(Joseph F. Smith, *Teachings of Presidents of the Church: Joseph F. Smith,* 32)

OCTOBER 9
Persecution

Tuesday, 9 Oct. 1838: The Prophet Joseph Smith, who has entered DeWitt, Missouri, to assist the beleaguered Saints there, determines that retreat in the face of vicious mob action is the only option available. The govenor sends word that the mob and "Mormons" should simply fight it out. Subsequently, property is destroyed. "The Saints were forbidden to go out of the town under pain of death, and were shot at when they attempted to go out to get food, of which they were destitute." The community is kept under constant cannon fire. "Some of the brethren perished from starvation. . . . These were men, too, who were virtuous and against whom no legal process could for one moment be sustained, but who, in consequence of their love of God, attachment to His cause, and their determination to keep the faith, were thus brought to an untimely grave" (*HC* 158–159). Two days later, the Prophet oversees the retreat of the Saints to neighboring Caldwell County, they having no hope of restitution for their losses, but retaining their faith, their hope, their virtue, and their prayers.

OCTOBER 10
Faith

Thursday, 10 Oct. 1833: While the Prophet Joseph Smith is away from Kirtland on a brief mission to the East and to Canada, Frederick G. Williams, a member of the First Presidency since March 1833 (*HC* 1:334), carries on the administrative work of the Church. This day he writes a heartfelt letter to the Saints in Missouri. Mail from Missouri had been diverted by the enemies of the Church, so he solicits and sends information through protected channels, and makes this statement: "We can do no more for you than we are doing; but we have this great consolation, that God will deliver Zion, and establish you upon the land of your everlasting inheritance. Remember that this is only for the trial of your faith, and he that overcomes and endures to the end, will be rewarded a hundred fold in this world, and in the world to come will receive eternal life; so brethren, you have great reason to rejoice, for your redemption draweth nigh" (*HC* 1:418).

OCTOBER 11
Parents

Sunday, 11 Oct. 1835: Joseph Smith has been caring for his sick father for several days. He reports this day: "[I] waited on my father again, who was very sick. In secret prayer in the morning, the Lord said, 'My servant, thy father shall live.' I waited on him all this day with my heart raised to God in the name of Jesus Christ, that He would restore him to health, that I might be blessed with his company and advice, esteeming it one of the greatest earthly blessings to be blessed with the society of parents, whose mature years and experience render them capable of administering the most wholesome advice" (*HC* 2:289). Such is the tenderness and petitions to heaven that Joseph often gave over his family members.

"It is one of the greatest blessings that God ever bestowed upon children that they have had parents who were in possession of true principles in relation to their Heavenly Father, salvation, eternal life, and were qualified and capable of teaching and traditionating their children in the sense that they may be qualified to fulfil the object of their creation."

(Wilford Woodruff, *Discourses of Wilford Woodruff*, 266)

OCTOBER 12
Missionary Work

Saturday, 12 Oct. 1833: The Prophet receives a great missionary revelation (Section 100) while he and Sidney Rigdon are serving a short-term proselyting mission to New York and Canada (*HC* 1:419–421). The Lord encapsulates the purpose for their mission in one phrase: "for the salvation of souls" (D&C 100:4). He promises that if they will lift up their voices, "it shall be given you in the very hour, yea, in the very moment, what ye shall say" (vv. 5–6).

"I know that member missionary work can be challenging. . . . [But these] three simple things . . . [can] . . . assist in this . . . responsibility. First, we should exercise our faith and pray . . . asking for help in finding ways to share the restored gospel. . . . Second, leaders must lead by example. . . . Third, member missionary work does not require the development of strategies or gimmicks. It does require faith—real faith and trust in the Lord. It also requires genuine love."

(M. Russell Ballard, *Ensign,* May 2003, 38–39)

OCTOBER 13
Hope Despite Death

Friday, 13 Oct. 1837: Jerusha Barden Smith dies at Kirtland while her husband, Hyrum, is away in Far West, Missouri, conducting affairs of the Church. Joseph Smith recalls, "She left five small children and numerous relatives to mourn her loss; her demise was severely felt by all. She said to one of her tender offspring when on her dying bed, 'Tell your father when he comes that the Lord has taken your mother home and left you for him to take care of' (*HC* 2:519). Sister Smith was one of the first to accept the testimony of her brother-in-law Joseph and was baptized at the same time as the Prophet's siblings William, Don Carlos, and Katherine, in June 1830. Having remained true and faithful to the gospel throughout her life, she left a noble legacy to her family. Her loved ones took comfort from Joseph's knowledge that "she died in full assurance of a part in the first resurrection" (*HC* 2:519).

"I never attend a funeral of a faithful member of the Church but I thank the Lord for the gospel of Jesus Christ, and for the comfort and consolation that it gives to us in the hour of sorrow and death."

(Heber J. Grant, *Gospel Standards,* 24–25)

OCTOBER 14

Love

Sunday, 14 Oct. 1838: Seven days after the Saints were driven from DeWitt, in Carroll County, Missouri, the Prophet ponders reports that some 800 ruthless mobbers are preparing to attack the Saints in Adam-ondi-Ahman in Davies County, to the northwest, and seize their property. So what does he teach in his Sabbath sermon? "I preached to the brethren at Far West from the saying of the Savior: 'Greater love hath no man than this, that he lay down his life for his brethren.'" He then calls for volunteers to join with him on the town square the next day to form a lawful militia, under proper state authority, "in strict accordance with the constitutional laws of the land" (*HC* 3:162), for the purpose of protecting the Saints to the north.

"One does not need to be killed in battle or die as a martyr in order to give one's life for one's friends. That man who lives out his years working for the uplift, the betterment, and the salvation of others . . . sacrificing his time, his strength, his means for others . . . also gives his life for his friends."

(J. Reuben Clark, Jr., *Improvement Era*, 39:661)

OCTOBER 15
Accountability

Sunday, 15 Oct. 1843: Joseph Smith preaches at Sunday services regarding the Constitution, the Bible, and economics. He begins: "I am the greatest advocate of the Constitution of the United States there is on the earth. . . . The only fault I find with the Constitution is, it is not broad enough to cover the whole ground" (*HC* 6:56–57). Elaborating on what he sees as a deficiency in that celebrated document, the Prophet continues: "Although it provides that all men shall enjoy religious freedom, yet it does not provide the manner by which that freedom can be preserved, nor for the punishment of Government officers who refuse to protect the people in their religious rights, or punish those mobs, states, or communities who interfere with the rights of the people on account of their religion. . . ." (*HC* 6:57).

OCTOBER 16
Falsehood

Thursday, 16 Oct. 1834: The Prophet Joseph and others leave Kirtland to visit the Saints in Michigan. During the boat trip across the lake, Oliver Cowdery strikes up a conversation with a passenger by the name of Ellmer, who claims to be "acquainted with Joe Smith, had heard him preach his lies, and now, since he was dead, [the man] was glad" (*HC* 2:168–169). The man goes on to claim he had heard Joseph preach in Bainbridge, New York and remembered him as a dark-complexioned fellow. Though all of the statements are untrue, the Prophet chooses to remain silent, later stating, "I am suffering under the tongue of slander for Christ's sake, unceasingly. God have mercy on such, if they will quit their lying" (*HC* 2:168–169).

"Joseph F Smith . . . was the target of vile accusations. . . . Listen to his response . . . 'Let them alone . . . give them the liberty of speech they want. . . .' At the time of his death, many of those who had ridiculed him wrote tributes of praise concerning him."

(Gordon B Hinckley, *Ensign,* Jun. 1991,4)

OCTOBER 17
Good Works

Thursday, 17 Oct. 1839: Five very ill missionaries left Nauvoo for England about a month earlier and now arrive in Terre Haute, Indiana. Three of the Elders stay with Brother Nahum Milton Stow, while Elders Brigham Young and Heber C. Kimball remain at the home of a Dr. Modisett. We read: "In the evening, Doctor Modisett went down to see the brethren, and appeared to be very much affected to see them so sick, and having to lie upon the floor on a straw bed. . . . When the doctor returned home, he told Elders Young and Kimball, he could not refrain from shedding tears to see the brethren going upon such a long mission, and in such suffering circumstances" (*HC* 4:15). In response, Elders Young and Kimball suggest that he "might have relieved them from 'their suffering and indigent circumstances upon their long mission'" (*HC* 4:15) by using some of his vast wealth (which he had described to them in some detail) to ease their burdens.

"You know very well that it is against my doctrine and feelings for men to scrape together the wealth of the world and let it waste and do no good."

(Brigham Young, *Discourses of Brigham Young*, 312)

OCTOBER 18
Hope

Thursday, 18 Oct. 1838: The Prophet's sister-in-law, Agnes Smith, is driven out into a snowstorm by a mob who plunder and burn her house. While her husband Don Carlos, brother of the Prophet, is away on a mission for the Church in Tennessee, she is forced to walk three miles, her two tiny infants in arm, and then wade across a river to safety. The Prophet writes in his journal: "Women and children, some in the most delicate condition, were thus obliged to leave their homes and travel several miles in order to effect their escape. My feelings were such as I cannot describe when I saw them flock into the village [Adam-ondi-Ahman, Missouri], almost entirely destitute of clothes, and only escaping with their lives" (*HC* 3:163). The state militia is called out to dispense the villains, but this is only a temporary solution (*HC* 3:164). For those who pressed on during these trials, the Lord's promise of a better world was probably often dreamed of.

"There are tremendous sources of hope beyond our own ability, learning, strength, and capacity. . . . 'Hope is the anchor of our souls.'"

(James E. Faust, *Ensign*, Nov. 1999, 59)

OCTOBER 19

Selfishness

Monday, 19 Oct. 1840: In the throes of the dire Missouri persecution and expulsion (1838–1839), the Prophet Joseph Smith and many of his colleagues were confined to various prisons under deplorable conditions of filth and squalor. Now, the following year, the Prophet and his brother Hyrum, looking back in a reflective mood, write from Nauvoo to the Saints in Kirtland, expressing concern and also reproving them for their previous silence: "Above all, for not sending one word of consolation to us while we were in the hands of our enemies, and thrust into dungeons. Some of our friends from various sections sent us letters which breathed a kind and sympathetic spirit, and which made our afflictions and sufferings endurable. All was silent as the grave [from Kirtland]; no feelings of sorrow, sympathy, or affection [was expressed] to cheer the heart under the gloomy shades of affliction and trouble through which we had to pass. . . . Where were the bowels of compassion? Where was the love which ought to characterize the Saints of the Most High?" (*HC* 4:225).

OCTOBER 20
Rights

Thursday, 20 Oct. 1842: On occasion, during the early years of intense persecution of the Church, the law stood up for the unjustly accused. On this day, Justin Butterfield, United States Attorney for the District of Illinois, provides an opinion letter to Sidney Rigdon concerning the attempt by ex-governor Boggs of Missouri to force Illinois to send Joseph Smith back to Missouri on charges of being an accessory to the attempted murder of Boggs. Butterfield explains in lucid language why this demand would be unconstitutional, i.e., because the Prophet was not in Missouri at the time of the crime and could not be considered a fugitive from justice (see *HC* 5:174). In Butterfield's opinion, "the supreme court [of Illinois] will discharge him upon habeas corpus" (*HC* 5:179). In this instance justice prevailed in the preservation of God-given constitutional rights—after the accused stood up politely for those rights, in accordance with due legal process.

OCTOBER 21
Holy Ghost

Wednesday, 21 Oct. 1840: Elder Lorenzo Snow, age 26, arrives this day in Manchester, England, from Nauvoo, beginning what will be a very fruitful mission of nearly three years' duration (*HC* 4:233; 5:353). Elder Snow sought a testimony in earnest prayer: "I had no sooner opened my lips in an effort to pray than I heard a sound just above my head like the rushing of silken robes; and immediately the Spirit of God descended upon me, completely enveloping my whole person, filling me from the crown of my head to the soles of my feet, and oh, the joyful happiness I felt! No language can describe the almost instantaneous transition from a dense cloud of spiritual darkness into a refulgence of light and knowledge, as it was at that time imparted to my understanding" (*HC* 4:162).

"A person may profit by noticing the first intimation of the spirit of revelation . . . so that by noticing it, you may find it fulfilled the same day or soon; . . . and thus by learning the Spirit of God and understanding it, you may grow into the principle of revelation, until you become perfect in Christ Jesus."

(Joseph Smith, *TPJS*, 151)

OCTOBER 22

Wholesome Recreation

Sunday, 22 Oct. 1837: The High Council and priesthood quorums in Kirtland take steps to elevate the social and recreational standards among members in the community, and to "commence the work of reform." The leaders consequently disfellowship twenty-two brethren and sisters "until they make satisfaction for uniting with the world in a dance the Thursday previous" (*HC* 2:519). The precise nature of the objectionable behavior at the dance is not recorded; however, the historical account shows a concerted effort to encourage "that unruly children be reported to their parents" (*HC* 2:520). From the very beginnings of the restored Church, the leaders took care to guide young people (and their parents) into wholesome channels of recreation, encouraging high standards of decorum even in recreational activities.

OCTOBER 23
Preparation

Tuesday, 23 Oct. 1838: The Prophet notes: "The word of the Lord was given several months since, for the Saints to gather into the cities, but they have been slow to obey until the judgments were upon them, and now they are gathering by flight and haste" (*HC* 3:166). In August of 1831 the Lord had counseled, concerning the Missouri settlements: "And let the work of the gathering be not in haste, nor by flight; but let it be done as it shall be counseled by the elders of the church at the conferences, according to the knowledge which they receive from time to time" (D&C 58:56). The Lord had counseled careful preparation, wise planning, orderly movement, and—above all—following the counsel of the Brethren. However, slothfulness now forced the people to move in undesired haste. The point is driven home when we recall that the extermination order was only four days away, and the massacre at Haun's Mill only one week away, the leaders there having turned a deaf ear to the Prophet's warning to gather to Far West.

OCTOBER 24
Gathering

Sunday, 24 Oct. 1841: Orson Hyde dedicates the Holy Land from the Mount of Olives (*HC* 4:456–459). Nine years previous, Elder Hyde had been blessed that "in due time thou shalt go to Jerusalem, the land of thy fathers, and be a watchman unto the house of Israel; and by thy hands shall the Most High do a great work, which shall prepare the way and greatly facilitate the gathering together of that people" (*HC* 4:375). In March 1840 he beheld a 6-hour vision of his coming mission: "The Spirit said unto me, 'Here are many of the children of Abraham whom I will gather to the land that I gave to their fathers; and here also is the field of your labors'" (*HC* 4:376).

Now, on October 24, in his eloquent apostolic dedicatory prayer, he consecrates the land "for the gathering together of Judah's scattered remnants, according to the predictions of the holy Prophets—for the building up of Jerusalem again after it has been trodden down by the Gentiles so long, and for rearing a Temple in honor of Thy name" (*HC* 4:456).

OCTOBER 25
Keep the Faith

Thursday, 25 Oct. 1838: At dawn, a patrol of militia from Far West, under command of Captain David W. Patten, acting by judicial order, makes its way toward the ford of Crooked River (20 miles distant), hoping to surprise an encampment of renegade mobbers. The mobbers, led by ruthless militiaman Samuel Bogart, had been terrorizing the Mormon settlers for several days, and had in fact kidnapped three brethren, whom they threatened to kill. Unfortunately, Patten's group is ambushed in the breaking rays of sunrise. Patten is fatally wounded and young Gideon Carter, a colleague, is killed instantly by a shot to the head (*HC* 3:171). Although the three captives are freed, Patten, one of the original Twelve, succumbs later that day, the first martyred Apostle of this dispensation. The Prophet wrote: "Brother David Patten was a very worthy man . . . and strong in the faith of a glorious resurrection, in a world where mobs will have no power or place. One of his last expressions to his wife was—'Whatever you do else, O! do not deny the faith'" (*HC* 3:171).

OCTOBER 26
Steadfastness

Monday, 26 Oct. 1835: Four Smith brothers—Joseph, Hyrum, Samuel H., and Don Carlos—are in court today to defend Samuel, who is accused of neglecting his military duty. He passes through another injustice and endures in faith. Another example of Samuel Harrison Smith's endurance can be found in his missionary efforts. He was instrumental in bringing Brigham Young and Heber C. Kimball into the Church. He died on July 30, 1844, just a month after the martyrdom of Joseph and Hyrum (*HC* 7:213). His obituary stated: "If ever there lived a good man upon the earth, Samuel H. Smith was that person. His labors in the church from first to last, carrying glad tidings to the eastern cities, and finally his steadfastness as one of the [eight special] *witnesses* to *the Book of Mormon,* and many saintly traits of virtue, knowledge, temperance, patience, godliness, brotherly kindness and charity, shall be given of him hereafter as a man of God" (*HC* 7:222).

OCTOBER 27
Heroes and Friends of God

Saturday, 27 Oct. 1838: On the same day as the funeral for Captain David W. Patten, the first martyred Apostle of this dispensation, Governor Lilburn W. Boggs of Missouri, reacting to inflammatory false reports of a "Mormon" insurrection against the state, orders General John B. Clark to mobilize the state militia for war (see *HC* 3:175). To Boggs, Elder Patten would be nothing but a murderer; to the Prophet Joseph Smith, calling at the home of the grieving family before the funeral, he is a hero: "There lies a man that has done just as he said he would—he has laid down his life for his friends" (*HC* 3:175). Elder Patten *had* given his life at the Battle of Crooked River while rescuing three brethren kidnapped by renegade militiamen.

"While we see this quality [submitting fully to the Lord] in the . . . lives of . . . spiritual heroes and heroines about us, lack of it keeps so many of us straggling in the foothills . . . of full discipleship. . . . A superficial view of this life . . . will not do."

(Neal A. Maxwell, *Ensign,* May 1985, 70–71)

OCTOBER 28
Knowledge

Wednesday, 28 Oct. 1840: A long communication from Heber C. Kimball, Wilford Woodruff, and George A. Smith arrives in Nauvoo detailing their missionary labors in London. A statement on the importance of gaining a correct knowledge of things is included: "We consider it perfectly consistent with our calling, with reason and revelation that we should form a knowledge of kingdoms and countries whether at home or abroad, whether ancient or modern, whether of things past or present or to come; whether it be in heaven, earth or hell, air or seas; or whether we obtain this knowledge by being local or traveling, by study or by faith, by dreams or by visions, by revelation or by prophecy, it mattereth not unto us; if we can but obtain a correct [view of] principles, and knowledge of things as they are, in their true light, past, present and to come" (*HC* 4:234).

"Knowledge is power, but the most vital and important knowledge is a knowledge of God. . . . All useful knowledge is of value. . . . But in all of our searching for truth, we must remember that the knowledge of God . . . is of supreme importance."

(Ezra Taft Benson, *Teachings of Ezra Taft Benson*, 293–294)

OCTOBER 29
Judge Not

Saturday, 29 Oct. 1842: The Prophet visits at his redbrick store with a group of Saints who had just arrived from New York. He prepares them to settle in Nauvoo with a proper attitude: "I showed them that it was generally in consequence of the brethren disregarding or disobeying counsel that they became dissatisfied and murmured; and many when they arrived here, were dissatisfied with the conduct of some of the Saints, because everything was not done perfectly right, and they get angry, and thus the devil gets advantage over them to destroy them. I told them I was but a man, and they must not expect me to be perfect; if they expected perfection from me, I should expect it from them; but if they would bear with my infirmities and the infirmities of the brethren, I would likewise bear with their infirmities" (*HC* 5:181).

OCTOBER 30
Safety

Tuesday, 30 Oct. 1838: At around 4 P.M. on this day of infamy, a mob assaults the families residing at the village of Haun's Mill—killing at least 17 (*HC* 3:182–188). Eyewitness Amanda Smith remarked of the horrific scene that "the groans of the wounded and dying were enough to have melted the heart of anything but a Missouri mob" (*HC* 3:324). The grieving Joseph Smith had warned all the Saints to gather to Adam-ondi-Ahman or Far West for safety, but Jacob Haun and others had decided to remain with their property. "Up to this day God had given me wisdom to save the people who took counsel," said the Prophet. "None had ever been killed who abode my counsel. At Haun's Mill the brethren went contrary to my counsel; if they had not, their lives would have been spared" (*HC* 5:137). What may be the Haun's Mill issue of our day?

OCTOBER 31
God's Inexorable Will

Wednesday, 31 Oct. 1838: The Missouri State Militia holds the settlement of Far West under siege. The Church leaders are taken prisoner and subjected during the night to severe abuse and an illegal court-martial, in which they are sentenced to be shot. In the words of Parley P. Pratt: "If the vision of the infernal regions could suddenly open to the mind, with thousands of malicious fiends, all clamoring, exulting, deriding, blaspheming, mocking, railing, raging and foaming like a troubled sea, then could some idea be formed of the hell which we had entered" (*HC* 3:189). Joseph and his colleagues are marched off to Richmond and eventually Liberty Jail. Though such evil and illegal acts eventually lead to the Prophet's death, the kingdom of God continued on—despite the expectations of the Church's enemies.

"What is Boggs or his murderous party, but wimbling willows upon the shore to catch the flood-wood? . . . Hell may pour forth its rage like the burning lava of mount Vesuvius . . . and yet shall 'Mormonism' stand."

(Joseph Smith, *HC* 3:297)

NOVEMBER

Therefore, verily, thus saith the Lord,
let Zion rejoice, for this is Zion—THE

PURE IN HEART . . .

—D&C 97:21

NOVEMBER 1
Warning

Tuesday, 1 Nov. 1831: A special conference convenes in Hiram, Ohio, to consider the publication of the "Book of Commandments" (predecessor to the Doctrine & Covenants). Joseph Smith inquires of the Lord for confirmation of the conference's decisions and receives what is now Section 1, the Lord's "preface unto the book of my commandments" (D&C 1:6; see *HC* 1:221–224). The theme of this revelation (and indeed of the book as a whole) is "the voice of warning" (v. 4). The Lord's plan is to cause men to trust in Him (rather than in the arm of flesh), to cause faith to increase, to establish His everlasting covenant and His Church, and to give all the inhabitants of the earth a chance to repent and prepare for the Second Coming of the Lord.

"Because the Lord is kind, He calls servants to warn people of danger. That call to warn is made harder and more important by the fact that the warnings of most worth are about dangers that people don't yet think are real."

(Henry B. Eyring, *Ensign,* Nov. 1998, 32–33)

NOVEMBER 2
Family

Friday, 2 Nov. 1838: Persecution and militia action against the Saints in northern Missouri reached a fevered pitch in October and November, 1838. The Prophet is torn from his family for transport to Independence and then on to Richmond, to face trial and possible execution. Reflecting on the event, he shares the tender feelings he has for his family. "Who can realize the feelings which I experienced at that time, to be thus torn from my companion, and leave her surrounded with monsters in the shape of men, and my children, too, not knowing how their wants would be supplied; while I was to be taken far from them in order that my enemies might destroy me when they thought proper to do so. My partner wept, my children clung to me, until they were thrust from me by the swords of the guards. I felt overwhelmed while I witnessed the scene, and could only recommend them to the care of [God]" (*HC* 3:193).

"We come to this earth charged with a mission: to learn to love and serve one another. To best help us accomplish this, God has placed us in families."

(John H. Groberg, *Ensign*, May 1982, 50)

NOVEMBER 3
Second Coming

Thursday, 3 Nov. 1831: Section 133 is received in Hiram, Ohio (*HC* 1:229–234). Like Section 1, the Lord's "preface," given two days earlier, this section offers a magnificent panorama of the great latter-day work. Its emphasis is on preparing for the Second Coming, fleeing from Babylon, gathering to Zion (or to Jerusalem, in the case of the people "of Judah"—v. 13), and generally looking forward in righteousness to the glorious events of the future. The culminating events attending the Savior's return are given in graphic detail: "And the Lord shall be red in his apparel, and his garments like him that treadeth in the wine-vat. And so great shall be the glory of his presence that the sun shall hide his face in shame, and the moon shall withhold its light, and the stars shall be hurled from their places" (vv. 48–49). The divine counsel: "Watch, therefore, for ye know neither the day nor the hour" (v. 11).

NOVEMBER 4
Testimony

Sunday, 4 Nov. 1838: The Prophet Joseph Smith preaches an unusual sermon while being marched toward Independence under extermination orders. A number of local citizens had come up to satisfy their curiosity. As the Prophet later records in his journal, one of the women in the group turned "to me [and] inquired whether I professed to be the Lord and Savior? I replied, that I professed to be nothing but a man, and a minister of salvation, sent by Jesus Christ to preach the Gospel. This answer so surprised the woman that she began to inquire into our doctrine, and I preached a discourse, both to her and her companions, and to the wondering soldiers, who listened with almost breathless attention while I set forth the doctrine of faith in Jesus Christ, and repentance, and baptism for remission of sins, with the promise of the Holy Ghost, as recorded in the second chapter of the Acts of the Apostles. The woman was satisfied, and praised God in the hearing of the soldiers, and went away, praying that God would protect and deliver us" (*HC* 3:200–201).

NOVEMBER 5
Deliverance

Tuesday, 5 Nov. 1833: November 5th and 6th mark the final flight of the Saints from Jackson County, Missouri. Lyman Wight reports, "I saw one hundred and ninety women and children driven thirty miles across the prairie in the month of November, with three decrepit men only in their company; the ground was thinly crusted with sleet, and I could easily follow on their trail by the blood that flowed from their lacerated feet on the stubble of the burnt prairie" (*HC* 1:438–439). He recounts further the tragic loss of two more women, Sarah Ann Higbee and Keziah Higbee, the latter after giving birth to a son on the banks of the river (*HC* 1:439–440). Yet through the deliverance of a loving God, the surviving Saints and their children would live to see a better day, and the restored Church would rise from the foundations of sacrifice to become a light for a world.

"Our safety lies in the virtue of our lives. Our strength lies in our righteousness. God has made it clear that if we will not forsake Him, He will not forsake us."

(Gordon B. Hinckley, *Ensign,* Nov. 2001, 90)

NOVEMBER 6
Living Prophets

Friday, 6 Nov. 1835: Joseph Smith is introduced to a man from the eastern part of the country: "After hearing my name, he remarked that I was nothing but a man, indicating by this expression, that he had supposed that a person to whom the Lord should see fit to reveal His will, must be something more than a man. He seemed to have forgotten the saying that fell from the lips of St. James, that Elias was a man subject to like passions as we are, yet he had such power with God, that He, in answer to his prayers, shut the heavens that they gave no rain for the space of three years and six months; and again, in answer to his prayer, the heavens gave forth rain, and the earth gave forth fruit [James 5:17–18]. Indeed, such is the darkness and ignorance of this generation, that they look upon it as incredible that a man should have any [communion] with his Maker" (*HC* 2:302).

"The Church is founded on continuing revelation to a current, living prophet. . . . Beginning with Joseph Smith and continuing on to his successors . . . the ongoing stream of revelation has perfected our understanding of the gospel."

(Merrill C. Oaks, *Ensign,* Nov. 1998, 83)

NOVEMBER 7
Faultfinding

Sunday, 7 Nov. 1841: The Prophet Joseph Smith takes a priesthood holder to task for his two-hour sermon reproving the Saints for "a lack of sanctity, and a want of holy living" (*HC* 4:445). The Prophet encourages an alternative approach, one designed to edify: "I charged the Saints not to follow the example of the adversary in accusing the brethren, and said, 'If you do not accuse each other, God will not accuse you. If you have no accuser you will enter heaven, and if you will follow the revelations and instructions which God gives you through me, I will take you into heaven as my back load. If you will not accuse me, I will not accuse you. If you will throw a cloak of charity over my sins, I will over yours—for charity covereth a multitude of sins" (*HC* 4:445).

"None of us is perfect; all of us occasionally make mistakes. . . . Men and women who carry heavy responsibility do not need criticism, they need encouragement. . . ."

(Gordon B. Hinckley, *Teachings of Gordon B. Hinckley*, 150)

NOVEMBER 8
Temple Work

Monday, 8 Nov. 1841: The baptismal font of the Nauvoo Temple is dedicated by Brigham Young, with the Prophet Joseph Smith in attendance. The first baptism for the dead in this dispensation had been performed on August 15, 1840 in the Mississippi River, with others following over the next few weeks (see *CHFT*, 251). On January 19, 1841, the Lord commanded that a temple be built for this purpose: "For this ordinance belongeth to my house, and cannot be acceptable to me, only in the days of your poverty, wherein ye are not able to build a house unto me" (D&C 124:30). On October 3, 1841, the Prophet announced that the Lord had commanded that no further baptisms for the dead be performed until they could be attended to in the temple (*HC* 4:426).

"The myriads of dead that have slept in the silent tomb without a knowledge of the gospel have their eyes upon us, and they are expecting us to fulfil the duties and responsibilities that devolve upon us to attend to, in which they are interested."

(John Taylor, *Teachings of Presidents of the Church: John Taylor*, 188–189)

NOVEMBER 9
Fellowship

Friday, 9 Nov. 1838: Following betrayal, narrow escape from execution, and a march to Richmond for trial, the Prophet and several colleagues suffer the following indignity in an abandoned house: "[They] ordered a man . . . to chain us together with chains and padlocks, being seven in number" (*HC* 3:206). The irony of forcing the prisoners to be bound together is that no earthly authority could deploy bonds to match the immovable covenant of fellowship that unites faithful Saints. The prisoners would never have abandoned each other. Just as the shackles they bore, and even the eventual death of the prophet, could not scatter the Saints and end their cause or association, earthly prison shackles, reminiscent of Satan's methods—"he had a great chain in his hand, and it veiled the whole face of the earth with darkness" (Moses 7:26)—cannot prevail against the sealing influence of divine authority.

NOVEMBER 10
Patience

Saturday, 10 Nov. 1838: The Saints in Adam-ondi-Ahman learn that they will be forced, yet again, to abandon their homes and farms: "As for their flocks and herds, the mob had relieved them from the trouble of taking care of them, or from the pain of seeing them starve to death—by stealing them. . . . About thirty of the brethren have been killed, many wounded, about a hundred are missing, and about sixty at Richmond awaiting their trial—for what they know not" (*HC* 3:207–208). In the midst of such severe trials, the Saints have no recourse but to persevere in patience and faith, with hope eternal that the Lord would lead them toward more secure pastures.

"Tribulation, afflictions, and trials will constantly be with us in our sojourn here in this segment of eternity, just as the Savior said, 'In the world ye shall have tribulation' (John 16:33). Therefore, the great challenge in this earthly life is not to determine how to escape the afflictions and problems, but rather to carefully prepare ourselves to meet them.

(Angel Abrea, *Ensign*, May 1992, 25)

NOVEMBER 11
Humility

Saturday, 11 Nov. 1843: The Prophet notes in his journal: "A company of Saints arrived from England. The work is still prospering in that country, poverty and distress are making rapid strides, and the situation of the laboring classes is getting every day more deplorable" (*HC* 6:71). By linking the progress of missionary work with the economic challenges confronting the people, the Prophet seems to be suggesting that increased humility renders people more receptive to spiritual truth. And so it is. The Apostle Peter said, "be clothed with humility: for God resisteth the proud, and giveth grace to the humble" (1 Pet. 5:5).

"We have all learned to be proud; anyone who doesn't think he is proud is very proud indeed. . . . There is no real hope for lasting improvement for those who refuse to humble themselves."

(Richard Chidester, *Ensign,* Mar. 1990, 19)

NOVEMBER 12
Spiritual Nourishment

Thursday, 12 Nov. 1835: The Prophet meets in Kirtland with the Quorum of the Twelve during the evening and delivers a discourse containing many gems of instruction to nourish their souls, calculated to prepare them for the coming endowment—an even greater spiritual feast. "Do not watch for iniquity in each other, if you do you will not get an endowment, for God will not bestow it on such. But if we are faithful, and live by every word that proceeds forth from the mouth of God, I will venture to prophesy that we shall get a blessing that will be worth remembering. . . . You need an endowment, brethren, in order that you may be prepared and able to overcome all things" (*HC* 2:308–309).

"Just as there is food for the body, there is food for the spirit. The consequences of spiritual malnutrition are just as hurtful to our spiritual lives as physical malnutrition is to our physical bodies. Symptoms of spiritual malnutrition include reduced ability to digest spiritual food, reduced spiritual strength, and impairment of spiritual vision. . . ."

(Dallin H. Oaks, *Ensign*, Dec. 1998, 7)

NOVEMBER 13

Truth

Monday, 13 Nov. 1843: The Prophet receives a thought-provoking letter from his non-Mormon acquaintance, General James Arlington Bennett, and responds the same day with inspiration that defies his lack of formal education (*HC* 6:71–78). Bennett raises two interesting points: Joseph Smith's success makes him "the most extraordinary man of the present age" (*HC* 6:72) and that spiritual matters are not subject to mathematical solutions. The Prophet responds to these points with gentle reproof. Point 1: Taking no credit for his accomplishments, the Prophet says only, "It demonstrates the fact that truth is mighty and must prevail, and that one man empowered from Jehovah has more influence with the children of the kingdom than eight hundred millions [i.e., the whole world] led by the precepts of men" (*HC* 6:74). Point 2: On proving spiritual matters, the Prophet adduces the "unimpeached" testimony of countless witnesses to the truth of the Bible and quotes from John 7:17 (see *HC* 6:77).

"The things of God are only to be discerned by the Spirit of God."

(Orson F. Whitney, CR, Apr. 1911, 48)

Monday, 14 Nov. 1842: Joseph Smith, as mayor of Nauvoo, presides at the city council where the "Ordinance regulating the proceedings on writs of habeas corpus" is passed (*HC* 5:185–192). The Latin phrase "habeas corpus" means "Thou (shalt) have the body." Such a writ requires that a person or persons restrained of liberty in some official manner, such as through arrest or imprisonment, be brought before the court (in this case the municipal court at Nauvoo) so that the legality of the restraint may be determined. The habeas corpus provision had proven decisive in saving the Prophet from extradition to Missouri when he was falsely arrested by lawmen from that state (for the second time) on August 8, 1842. Thus the leaders of the Church, while extending the tent of Zion to secure to their faithful people every possible spiritual blessing from the Lord, also extend the canopy of the Constitution to protect their people from the encroachments of evil men seeking to destroy their temporal rights and privileges.

NOVEMBER 15

Endurance

Monday, 15 Nov. 1841: An important epistle from the Twelve is sent this day to the Saints abroad among whom they had labored. They counsel that gathering not be done in haste, but with prudence, as circumstance and means permit. While expatiating on the grand opportunities for land and commerce in America, they remind emigrants to expect to be tried in the crucible of adversity, with constant challenges from the enemies of the Church: "The wheat and tares must grow together till the harvest; at the harvest the wheat is gathered together into the threshing floor, so with the Saints—the stakes are the threshing floor. Here they will be threshed with all sorts of difficulties, trials, afflictions and everything to mar their peace, which they can imagine, and thousands which they cannot imagine, but he that endures the threshing till all the chaff, superstition, folly and unbelief are pounded out of him, and does not suffer himself to be blown away as chaff by the foul blast of slander, but endures faithfully to the end, shall be saved" (*HC* 4:451–452).

NOVEMBER 16
Forgiveness

Monday, 16 Nov. 1835: The Prophet Joseph Smith receives a letter from an inactive elder by the name of Harvey Whitlock, who petitions for forgiveness of his sins and asks the Prophet to inquire of the Lord concerning his case. Says he, "For I am willing to receive any chastisement that the Lord sees I deserve" (*HC* 2:314). Moved to tears over the penitent spirit of this prodigal son, the Prophet immediately inquires of the Lord and receives a revelation. Excerpt: "Verily, thus saith the Lord unto you—Let him who was my servant Harvey, return unto me . . . and forsake all the sins wherewith he has offended against me, and pursue from henceforth a virtuous and upright life. . . . And behold, saith the Lord your God, his sins shall be blotted out from under heaven . . . and he shall be exalted" (*HC* 2:315).

"Instead of dwelling on the wickedness and grief of those who have sinned, I rejoice to read how many have abandoned their sinful practices and are now on the road back to righteousness and happiness. . . . Let us . . . rejoice in the spirit of forgiveness, which is the comforting message of the Atonement."

(Theodore M. Burton, *Ensign,* May 1983, 71–72)

NOVEMBER 17
Good Literature

Sunday, 17 Nov. 1839: During this month the newspaper *Times & Seasons* is launched in Nauvoo (*HC* 4:23). As the Church's official publication, it is used to communicate important doctrinal materials, articles and discourses from priesthood leaders, information about the history and progress of the Restoration, and excerpts from the books of Moses and Abraham. As the *Ensign* of its day, the *Times & Seasons* played a vital role in contributing to the enlightenment of the Saints and the welding together of a unified community of believers.

"Unfortunately, we live now in a sex-saturated society. Pornography comes at us from all sides. . . . There is no way to blank it out entirely. But we can do something to offset its corrosive influence. We can expose our children to good reading. Let them grow with good books and good Church magazines around them. Have handy the weekly *Church News,* which will bring to them the feeling that they belong to a great, viable, vital organization that moves across the world, affecting the lives of men and women for good in many lands."

(Gordon B. Hinckley, *Ensign,* May 1982, 42)

NOVEMBER 18
Conversion

Thursday, 18 Nov. 1830: Parley P. Pratt and others complete a short but successful missionary journey through the Western Reserve area of Ohio (the northeastern section) during the month of November 1830 (*HC* 1:120–125; *CHFT*, 81–82). Within just a few weeks, using the Book of Mormon as an instrument of conversion, they are able to baptize 127 persons, including Lyman Wight, John Murdock, and Sidney Rigdon. The latter was a minister with a considerable circle of followers in the Kirtland/Mentor vicinity, many of whom embraced the gospel. In the fall of 1865, Rigdon was visited by his son, John, who asked his father to confirm his testimony of the Book of Mormon. Sidney Rigdon replied, "My son, I can swear before high heaven that what I have told you about the origin of that book is true" (*HC* 1:123).

"We must understand why this inspired book of scripture is the heart of missionary proselyting. Conversion to it is conversion to Christ, because this book contains the words of Christ."

(Joseph B. Wirthlin, *Ensign,* Sep. 2002, 14)

NOVEMBER 19
Renewal

Monday, 19 Nov. 1848: An arsonist sets fire to the Nauvoo Temple. The *Nauvoo Patriot* reports: "On Monday the 19th of November, our citizens were awakened by the alarm of fire, which, when first discovered, was bursting out through the spire of the Temple. . . . The materials of the inside were so dry, and the fire spread so rapidly, that a few minutes were sufficient to wrap this famed edifice in a sheet of flame. It was a sight too full of mournful sublimity. . . . and men looked on with faces sad as if the crumbling ruins below were consuming all their hopes" (*HC* 7:617–618). The majority of the Saints had already abandoned the City of Joseph (Nauvoo) and left the building in the hands of the Lord upon their departure to the West. Subsequently, on May 27, 1850, the exterior walls of the Temple were demolished by a tornado (see *CHFT*, 242).

"[I] feel impressed to announce that among all of the temples we are constructing, we plan to rebuild the Nauvoo Temple. . . . The new building will stand as a memorial to those who built the first such structure."

(Gordon B. Hinckley, *Ensign,* May 1999, 89)

NOVEMBER 20
Kindness

Monday, 20 Nov. 1843: Look in upon a family home evening, Nauvoo style. Joseph's journal records: "Two gentlemen from Vermont put up at the Mansion. I rode around with them in the afternoon to show them the improvements in the city. In the evening, several of the Twelve and others called to visit me. My family sang hymns, and Elder John Taylor prayed and gave an address, to which they paid great attention, and seemed very much interested" (*HC* 6:79–80). The Prophet of the Restoration as host; several Apostles in attendance, one of whom speaks and prays; and the Prophet's family providing the music. No wonder the two visitors pay close attention. The whole event reflects the Prophet's social graces and hospitality toward visitors to Nauvoo, the "beautiful" city.

"I pray that the love of the gospel of our Lord will . . . cause husbands to be kinder to wives, and wives to be kinder to husbands, parents to children, and children to parents . . . It will cause us . . . to love our neighbors as ourselves . . . If possible, to help them understand better the purpose of life."

(George Albert Smith, *The Teachings of George Albert Smith*, 136)

NOVEMBER 21
Preserving Liberty

Tuesday, 21 Nov. 1843: Joseph "dictated to [his] clerk an appeal to the Green Mountain boys of Vermont, [his] native State" (*HC* 6:80) for their support in stopping Missouri injustice against the Saints. The Prophet refers to Ethan Allen's famous "Green Mountain Boys," who gained fame for their capture of Fort Ticonderoga from the British early in the Revolutionary War. The Prophet opens: "I was born in Sharon, Vermont. . . . My fathers . . . fought and bled; and with the most of that venerable band of patriots, they have gone to rest, bequeathing a glorious country, with all her inherent rights, to millions of posterity" (*HC* 6:88). This sacrifice was to secure all citizens' inalienable rights. "But, to the disgrace of the United States," Joseph wrote, "it is not so" (*HC* 6:89).

"[We believe in] preserving life and liberty. . . . [Those] called to serve in [this] cause . . . may enter into battle with confidence that so long as [they are] righteous . . . if death overtakes [them] on the field of battle . . . [they] will be recieved by that God who gave them life."

(William E. Berret, *A Book of Mormon Treasury*, 284)

NOVEMBER 22
Songs of Praise

Sunday, 22 Nov. 1835: During this month, the hymnal prepared by Emma Smith is published. This important publication included the words to 90 hymns (34 of which were written by members of the Church). Musical notation was not included in this hymnal; the words were sung by the congregation to well-known melodies of the day (see *CHFT*, 153, 161–162). A second and enlarged edition was published in 1841 (see *Doctrine and Covenants Student Manual*, 52). Music played a central and divinely instituted role in the social and spiritual life of the Saints.

"In my traveling among the Saints, I have observed . . . a disposition to displace the Latter-day Saint hymns with sectarian songs. . . . I suppose that some . . . would say that these hymns are old . . . The gospel of the Lord Jesus Christ, is not new. . . . Do we love our fathers and our mothers less because of their age, because they are getting old? No; and I tell you that these hymns, which have been selected by inspiration from the Lord, they are never dying to the Latter-day Saints."

(George F. Richards, CR, Oct. 1911, 55–56)

NOVEMBER 23
Study of Faith

Sunday, 23 Nov. 1834: During the winter of 1834–35 the curriculum for the School of the Elders in Kirtland consisted of the "Lectures on Faith." These celebrated theological lectures were presented by Joseph Smith and Sidney Rigdon to the missionaries, who were encouraged to commit them to memory. "The classes, being mostly Elders gave the most studious attention to the all-important object of qualifying themselves as messengers of Jesus Christ, to be ready to do His will in carrying glad tidings to all that would open their eyes, ears and hearts" (*HC* 2:176; see *CHFT*, 124, 160–161).

"The Lord gave important instructions to seek balanced learning. The terms in the scriptures are *study* and *faith.* . . . To me, the terms *learning by study* and *learning by faith* say that self-reliance comes from both efforts. . . Because I was willing to study the gospel of Jesus Christ, I became a member of the Church and developed great faith in the Savior. My faith gave me more strength to seek knowledge by study. I cannot separate learning by study and learning by faith. Both of them touch my heart, enlighten my mind, and encourage me in service."

(Chieko N. Okazaki, *Ensign,* Nov. 1994, 92–93)

NOVEMBER 24
Marriage

Tuesday, 24 Nov. 1835: The Prophet Joseph Smith and his wife Emma attend a wedding at the home of Hyrum Smith, where the Prophet solemnizes the ceremony uniting Newel Knight and his bride Lydia Goldthwaite. The Prophet writes: "I then remarked that marriage was an institution of heaven, instituted in the garden of Eden; that it was necessary it should be solemnized by the authority of the everlasting Priesthood. . . . I then pronounced them husband and wife in the name of God, and also pronounced upon them the blessings that the Lord conferred upon Adam and Eve in the garden of Eden, that is, to multiply and replenish the earth, with the addition of long life and prosperity" (*HC* 2:320). Vital sealing ordinances had not yet been introduced to this dispensation, but the seeds of eternal love and commitment were planted when the solemn union of this couple commenced.

NOVEMBER 25
Children of Light

Tuesday, 25 Nov. 1834: Warren A. Cowdery, older brother of Oliver Cowdery, is called to be a presiding high priest in the community of Freedom, New York, and vicinity (Section 106), and is promised that if he will "devote his whole time to this high and holy calling. . . . seeking diligently the kingdom of heaven and its righteousness," then "all things necessary shall be added thereunto; for the laborer is worthy of his hire" (v. 3). It takes faith to depend so totally on the Lord. The Lord adds this admonition (reminiscent of Paul's inspired words, cited above): "Therefore, gird up your loins, that you may be the children of light, and that day shall not overtake you as a thief" (v. 5).

"We know that Jesus Christ is 'the light of the world' (John 8:12) . . . Christ also charges us . . . to be his disciples by bringing his light and love to others."

(Annette P. Bowen, *Ensign,* Jul. 1995, 56)

NOVEMBER 26
Honesty

Friday, 26 Nov. 1841: Hyrum Smith, Patriarch to the Church, issues an affidavit this day in response to reports accusing the First Presidency and other Church leaders of advocating that members should steal from nonmembers. Hyrum denounces this accusation in the strongest terms (see *HC* 4:460). The Prophet also responds by publishing in the *Times & Seasons* a "Denunciation of Thieves" saying, among other things: "I wish it to be distinctly understood . . . that the Church . . . will ever set its brows like brass, and its face like steel, against all such abominable acts of villainy and crime" (*HC* 4:462). No one could doubt how seriously the leadership of the Church took the issue. Roaming robber bands were at work stealing throughout the region and blaming it on the "Mormons."

"It is the responsibility of each of us to be . . . honest in our dealings and relationships, honest in our Church membership, honest in keeping the commandments of God."

(Delbert L. Stapley, *Ensign,* Jun. 1971, 104)

NOVEMBER 27
Safety

Wednesday, 27 Nov. 1839: While Joseph Smith is en route to Washington, D.C., to speak with President Van Buren and seek redress for the persecution of the Saints, the coachman, at a rest stop, steps away for a drink, and the horses run away at full speed with the crowded coach. "I persuaded my fellow travelers to be quiet and retain their seats," writes the Prophet in his journal, "[then] opening the door, I secured my hold on the side of the coach the best way I could, and succeeded in placing myself in the coachman's seat, and reining up the horses, after they had run some two or three miles, and neither coach, horses, or passengers received any injury" (*HC* 4:23). The Prophet was skillful in securing the safety of his colleagues. If we heed him, he will also secure our spiritual safety.

"There has always been a desperate need for the steady and reassuring voice of a living prophet of God: one who will speak the mind and will of God in showing the way to spiritual safety and personal peace and happiness."

(Robert D. Hales, *Ensign,* May 1995, 15)

NOVEMBER 28
The Book of Mormon

Sunday, 28 Nov. 1841: The Prophet Joseph Smith spends the day in dialogue with the Twelve Apostles at the home of Brigham Young. Even though the conversation covers "a variety of subjects," the Prophet chooses to memorialize in his journal only one of the themes: "I told the brethren that the Book of Mormon was the most correct of any book on earth, and the keystone of our religion, and a man would get nearer to God by abiding by its precepts, than by any other book" (*HC* 4:461).

"[The Book of Mormon] helps us draw nearer to God. Is there not something deep in our hearts that longs to draw nearer to God? . . . There is a power in the book which will begin to flow into your lives the moment you begin a serious study of the book. You will find greater power to resist temptation. You will find the power to avoid deception. You will find the power to stay on the strait and narrow path. The scriptures are called 'the words of life' (see D&C 84:85), and nowhere is that more true than it is of the Book of Mormon. When you begin to hunger and thirst after those words, you will find life in greater and greater abundance."

(Ezra Taft Benson, *Ensign,* Nov. 1986, 4–5)

NOVEMBER 29

Trust in the Lord

Friday, 29 Nov. 1839: This morning the Prophet Joseph Smith meets the president of the United States, Martin Van Buren. Later, on February 6, 1840, the Prophet summarizes this interview using the president's famous words: "*Gentlemen, your cause is just, but I can do nothing for you*" (*HC* 4:80). On March 4, 1840, Joseph writes: "May he never be elected again to any office of trust or power, by which he may abuse the innocent and let the guilty go free" (*HC* 4:89). Upon reflection, we realize our Lord and King is the opposite of President Van Buren. It is almost as if He says to us, "Your cause is unjust (as we are unprofitable servants), but I willingly do everything for you." Only He never abuses His position of trust, which is infinite and eternal.

NOVEMBER 30
Be Valiant

Friday, 30 Nov. 1838: Joseph Smith, Hyrum Smith, Sidney Rigdon, and several others are this day consigned to Liberty Jail. During the trial, William E. McLellin, one of the original Twelve Apostles, now excommunicated, sees fit to plunder the houses of several of the prisoners, and actually seeks permission from the sheriff to flog the Prophet. McLellin came to Parley P. Pratt during the trial and said, "Well, Parley, you have now got where you are certain never to escape; how do you feel as to the course you have taken in religion?" Elder Pratt: "I answered that I had taken the course which I should take if I had my life to live over again" (*HC* 3:215). These two apostles stood at opposite ends of the spectrum.

"Not to be valiant in one's testimony is a tragedy of eternal consequence. There are members who know this latter-day work is true, but who fail to endure to the end. . . . My appeal to all members of the Church is to be valiant—true and loyal."

(Ezra Taft Benson, *Ensign*, Feb. 1987, 2)

ECEMBER

The gathering together upon the land of Zion, and upon her stakes, may be for a defense, and for a refuge from the storm.

—D&C 115:6

DECEMBER 1

Boldness

Thursday, 1 Dec. 1831: Joseph Smith and Sidney Rigdon receive Section 71, a commandment to set aside, for a season, their translation of the Bible and instead preach the gospel in the communities round about. The purpose for this new campaign is to use the truth to counteract the negative publicity being engendered at the time by anti-Mormon articles being published by defector Ezra Booth (see *HC* 1:215–217, 238–239): "Wherefore, confound your enemies; call upon them to meet you both in public and in private; and inasmuch as ye are faithful their shame shall be made manifest. Wherefore, let them bring forth their strong reasons against the Lord. Verily, thus saith the Lord unto you—there is no weapon that is formed against you [that] shall prosper" (D&C 71:7–9). For the next five or six weeks they labor diligently, "setting forth the truth, vindica-ting the cause of our Redeemer; showing that the day of vengeance was coming upon this generation like a thief in the night" (*HC* 1:241). Thus we see that the truth, delivered in the boldness of the Spirit, establishes the Lord's kingdom.

DECEMBER 2
Loving-kindness of the Lord

Thursday, 2 Dec. 1841: The Prophet Joseph Smith receives a revelation on behalf of Nancy Marinda Hyde, wife of Orson Hyde, confirming the Lord's compassion toward the women of the Restoration whose husbands were serving on missions. In view of the burdens upon Sister Hyde during this long absence, the Lord decrees: "Behold it is my will that she should have a better place prepared for her, than that in which she now lives, in order that her life may be spared unto her; therefore go and say unto my servant, Ebenezer Robinson, and to my handmaid his wife—Let them open their doors and take her and her children into their house and take care of them faithfully and kindly until my servant Orson Hyde returns from his mission" (*HC* 4:467).

DECEMBER 3
Compassion

Sunday, 3 Dec. 1843: Malady and accidents wait for the convenience of no man. In the midst of priesthood gatherings, civic rallies, political upheaval, and important initiatives to counteract the injustices heaped upon the Saints by lawless executives, ill health makes its unwelcome entrance. Hyrum Smith suffers the effects of a severe leg injury sustained in a nasty fall, Emma Smith is battling a malaise that keeps her up through the night, and Nathan Pratt (Parley P. Pratt's son) is likewise taken ill. What does an over-burdened prophet do under such circumstances? Why, minister in person to the sick and pray for their recovery, of course. At the prayer meeting held in the upper chamber of the Prophet's redbrick store this afternoon, the assembled brethren offer a fervent prayer for all those who are sick at this time (see *HC* 6:98–99).

"He calls upon us to care for the sick, the poor, the afflicted; to pray for and show compassion towards all of God's children, for 'God is no respecter of persons' (Acts 10:34). With Him there are no barriers of race or gender or language."

(Alexander B. Morrison, *Ensign,* Nov. 1999, 25)

DECEMBER 4
Bishops

Sunday, 4 Dec. 1831: The Prophet receives Section 72 in the company of several of the Elders and members assembled to learn their duty and to be further edified (*HC* 1:239–241). The revelation calls Newel K. Whitney to be a bishop in the Kirtland area to handle the temporal and stewardship affairs of the Saints there. Additional duties of the bishop are outlined in the 72nd section: "To keep the Lord's storehouse; to receive the funds of the church in this part of the vineyard" (v.10), to administer to the needs of the Elders, care for the poor and needy, judge the worthiness of the Saints and recommend them "unto the bishop in Zion" (v. 17), and provide for the publication needs of the Church.

"[Bishops] are faithful men chosen by inspiration. . . . If any officer in the Church has my sympathy, it is the bishop. If any officer in the Church deserves credit for patience, for long-suffering, kindness, charity, and for love unfeigned, it is the bishop who does his duty. And we feel to sustain in our faith and love, the bishops and counselors in Zion."

(Joseph F. Smith, *Gospel Doctrine,* 157)

DECEMBER 5
Beware of Pride

Friday, 5 Dec. 1834: The Prophet Joseph Smith ordains Oliver Cowdery an "Assistant President of the Church" (*HC* 2:176). Oliver had been with the Prophet when the Aaronic and Melchizedek Priesthoods were restored, and would be with him during the glorious restoration of keys in the Kirtland Temple on April 3, 1836. How could the "second elder of this church" (D&C 20:3) and one of the Three Witnesses to the Book of Mormon later fall away and lose his membership in the Church? In a word: *pride*. He was excommunicated on April 12, 1838, for undermining the character and leadership of Joseph Smith, placing worldly business interests ahead of the kingdom of God, and "neglecting his high and holy calling" (*HC* 3:16). He was not rebaptized until 1848, and had to humble himself a great deal, pleading only for a position as the lowliest member.

DECEMBER 6
Servants as Saviors

Thursday, 6 Dec. 1832: While the Prophet is reviewing the manuscript of his inspired revision of the Bible, he is given the Lord's interpretation of the parable of the wheat and the tares (Section 86; see *HC* 1:300). The righteous who respond to the good word of the Lord through the Apostles are the wheat, while the tares represent those who respond to the wickedness of the world and the promptings of Satan. Through the restoration of the gospel, the tender blades are springing forth once again, but are threatened by the choking growth of the tares. The Lord restrains the angels of the harvest from plucking out the tares "while the blade is yet tender (for verily your faith is weak), lest you destroy the wheat also" (D&C 86:6). Instead, the reaping of the harvest is to wait for a time. The privilege of the children of Israel is to preach His gospel (see vv. 9–10), and thus expand the harvest of wheat by saving their fellowmen.

DECEMBER 7
Sustaining Leaders

Thursday, 7 Dec. 1843: A public meeting of the citizens of Nauvoo is held at 11 A.M. near the temple in support of the Prophet Joseph Smith, who continues to be the target of unlawful treatment at the hands of the authorities in Missouri. A resolution is drafted characterizing the Prophet as innocent of all offense, and "a good, industrious, well-meaning, and worthy citizen of Illinois, and an officer that does faithfully and impartially administer the laws of the State" (*HC* 6:102). The framers of the resolution declare that they "crave the protection of the Constitution and laws of the country as an *aegis* to shield him, the said General Joseph Smith, from such cruel persecutions" (*HC* 6:102) Thus the community rallies to the support of its leader in an hour of crisis, as it had done, and would do, on many other occasions.

"[It is our] privilege to sustain those in authority over us. . . . and let [only] God judge their actions. . . . I do not speak of blind obedience, but rather the obedience of faith, which supports and sustains decisions with confidence that they are inspired."

(James E. Faust, *Ensign,* May 1997, 42–43)

DECEMBER 8
Mission

Wednesday, 8 Dec. 1830: About this time Sidney Rigdon and Edward Partridge come to Fayette to meet Joseph Smith. The Prophet inquires of the Lord and receives a revelation for each of them. Edward is called to preach the gospel: "And I will lay my hand upon you by the hand of my servant Sidney Rigdon, and you shall receive my Spirit, the Holy Ghost, even the Comforter, which shall teach you the peaceable things of the kingdom; And you shall declare it with a loud voice, saying: Hosanna, blessed be the name of the most high God" (D&C 36:2–3).

"You have come to Earth at this time for a special purpose. He has a mission for you to accomplish, a *lifetime* mission. . . . Choose to stand with the Lord. Join with the valiant prophet Joshua, who declared, 'Choose you this day whom ye will serve . . . but as for me and my house, we will serve the Lord' (Josh. 24:15)."

(Russell C. Taylor, *Ensign,* May 1989, 40–42)

DECEMBER 9
Charity

Wednesday, 9 Dec. 1835: Joseph Smith is deeply touched by the charitable generosity of his friends and associates. Two of the local men cancel notes they are holding for money he owes them, and twenty others make contributions to him, totaling $64.50. "My heart swells with gratitude inexpressible when I realize the great condescension of my heavenly Father, in opening the hearts of these my beloved brethren to administer so liberally to my wants. And I ask God, in the name of Jesus Christ, to multiply blessings without number upon their heads" (*HC* 2:327).

"Christmas time with its cargo of love is the greatest of all anniversaries for those who worship the God of love. . . . It is the day when love takes command, and men, women, and children, by losing themselves, find joy and peace. For one day at least, Christendom tries Christianity. If this formula for happiness—love one another—is effective for one day, may it not work at other times, at all times?"

(Hugh B. Brown, *Continuing the Quest*, 463)

DECEMBER 10
Gratitude

Thursday, 10 Dec. 1835: On this beautiful winter day in Kirtland, a number of brethren meet to participate in a service project—chopping and hauling a supply of wood to carry the Prophet's family through the winter. The Prophet is deeply grateful. He asks the Lord for a blessing of grand scope upon his benefactors, guaranteeing health, wisdom, preservation, power over all their enemies, and "that they may journey to the land of Zion, and be established on their inheritances, to enjoy undisturbed peace and happiness forever, and ultimately be crowned with everlasting life in the celestial Kingdom of God" (*HC* 2:329).

"Where there is appreciation, there is courtesy, there is concern for the rights and property of others. Without appreciation, there is arrogance and evil. Where there is gratitude, there is humility, as opposed to pride. How magnificently we are blessed! How thankful we ought to be!"

(Gordon B. Hinckley, *Teachings of Gordon B. Hinckley*, 247)

DECEMBER 11
Record Keeping

Saturday, 11 Dec. 1841: The Prophet writes, "Since I have been engaged in laying the foundation of the Church of Jesus Christ of Latter-day Saints, I have been prevented in various ways from continuing my journal and history in a manner satisfactory to myself or in justice to the cause. . . . yet I have continued to keep up a journal in the best manner my circumstances would allow . . . as I have had opportunity so that the labors and suffering of the first Elders and Saints of this last kingdom might not wholly be lost to the world" (*HC* 4:470). "There are but few subjects," he wrote some two years later, "that I have felt a greater anxiety about than my history" (*HC* 6:66). Should not we, who have far fewer impediments to overcome, be equally anxious to record. After all, the history of the Church continues, and we are a part of it.

DECEMBER 12
Scriptures

Sunday, 12 Dec. 1830: As the Prophet Joseph Smith is at work on the inspired revision of the Bible, the Lord reveals to him significant material from the lost "Prophecy of Enoch," as mentioned in Jude, 1:14–15 and contained in the writings of Moses (*HC* 1:131–139). Note some of the glorious truths contained in these passages: (1) the significance of baptism as a rebirth (see Moses 6:60); (2) the nature of a Zion people and the city of Zion (see Moses 7:18–21); (3) the nature of Christ's atoning mission in bringing about sanctification and eternal life (see Moses 7:45–59); (4) the anguish of the Lord and his angels over the wickedness of His children, but also their joy over the righteous remnant (see Moses 7:37, 53); and (5) the bringing again of the translated city of Zion in the last days to meet the Lord's elect: "And the Lord said unto Enoch: Then shalt thou and all thy city meet them there, and we will receive them into our bosom, and they shall see us; and we will fall upon their necks . . . and we will kiss each other" (Moses 7:63).

DECEMBER 13
Consecration

Monday, 13 Dec. 1841: Brigham Young and his colleagues issue "An Epistle of the Twelve Apostles to the Saints of the Last Days" concerning the urgency of completing the Nauvoo Temple. The Twelve call for universal support in giving of one's time, talents, and resources to hasten the project along. The reasoning in this epistle has application to us today. A few examples: "No one is excepted who hath aught in his possession, for what have ye that ye have not received [from the Lord]?" (*HC* 4:472). "Many in this place are laboring every tenth day for the house, and this is the tithing of their income, for they have nothing else; others would labor the same, but they are sick, therefore excusable; when they get well, let them begin; while there are others who appear to think their own business of more importance than the Lord's. Of such we would ask, who gave you your time, health, strength, and put you into business?" (*HC* 4:473–474). All comes from the Lord; all should be offered in return.

DECEMBER 14
Gathering

Tuesday, 14 Dec. 1830: In this month, the Prophet Joseph Smith and Sidney Rigdon receive a revelation near Fayette, New York, in which the first commandment concerning a gathering in this dispensation is given: "And again, a commandment I give unto the church, that it is expedient in me that they should assemble together at the Ohio [Kirtland]" (D&C 37:3). The persecution against the Church in New York had become bitter, and it was the Lord's design to gather the Saints to Ohio for a season of time where the spirit was more conducive to the unfolding of the infant Church. We gather as families, wards, and stakes, and the whole Church gathers its forces to fulfill the functions of the Abrahamic Covenant.

"[The subject of the gathering] is a principle I esteem to be of the greatest importance . . . . All that the prophets that have written, from the days of righteous Abel, down to the last man that has left any testimony on record for our consideration, in speaking of the salvation of Israel in the last days, goes directly to show that it consists in the work of the gathering."

(Joseph Smith, *TPJS*, 83)

DECEMBER 15
Peacemaking

Tuesday, 15 Dec. 1835: Orson Hyde delivers a letter to Joseph Smith complaining that the Temple Committee (Hyrum Smith, Reynolds Cahoon, and Jared Carter) have acted inappropriately. When the Prophet misplaces this letter, Orson Hyde brings a copy to him two days later and reads the lengthy text aloud to him. The Prophet is unwell at the time, and still smarting from a verbal and physical attack that his brother William had unleashed on him in another context. Nevertheless, he listens patiently to Orson, then clarifies the facts in such a way that the two part company cheerfully with a handshake. The Prophet readily forgives him the ingratitude manifested in his letter, "knowing that it was for want of correct information" (*HC* 2:337). Then, concluding that the Temple Committee had indeed not acted appropriately in all things, the Prophet quietly takes steps to correct the situation with Elder Cahoon.

"The Lord . . . expects us to be peacemakers. He asks us to work out a reconciliation in a Christlike manner with those with whom we have difficulties or misunderstandings."

(O. Leslie Stone, *Ensign,* Nov. 1974, 32)

DECEMBER 16
Chastening

Monday, 16 Dec. 1833: Amid persecution and dislocation in Missouri, a revelation from the Lord (Section 101) informs the Saints: "Therefore, they must needs be chastened and tried, even as Abraham, who was commanded to offer up his only son. For all those who will not endure chastening, but deny me, cannot be sanctified" (vv. 4–5). The Lord assures that He will remember them, comfort them, gather them, and give them a crown. "Be still," He counsels, "and know that I am God" (v. 16). In an hour of great affliction, the Lord shows them that He is in charge of the flow of events, and reinforces the age-old pattern of righteousness: that all should repent, depend on Him, and humbly submit to divine chastening as a gateway to spiritual growth and ultimate victory.

"We soon find in this process of tutoring and mentoring that chastening may be involved. . . . The Lord tells us that He chastens those whom He loves. In fact, the chastened may be the only individuals willing so to learn (see Mosiah 23:21). . . . Christ often corrected before commending."

(Neal A. Maxwell, *Ensign*, Feb. 2001, 10–11)

DECEMBER 17
Mission in Life

Saturday, 17 Dec. 1842: Governor Ford of Illinois sends Joseph Smith a positive letter relative to the attempt by the governor of Missouri to have the Prophet extradited for trial: "They were unanimous in the opinion that the requisition from Missouri was illegal and insufficient to cause your arrest" (*HC* 5:205). Thus the Prophet, so often wrongfully accused and abused before the law, comes off this time the victor, and is spared but a little longer until he can faithfully complete his appointed mission on earth.

"We need to see all of life as one great mission. . . . We must stop trying to separate missionary work from life. Missionary work is life—living is a mission; life is a mission."

(John H. Groberg, *Ensign*, Jul. 1980, 9)

DECEMBER 18
Loving Correction

Friday, 18 Dec. 1835: The Prophet receives a letter of confession and apology from his younger brother William (then 28 years old), who had "used violence" against Joseph and others (including Hyrum) at a meeting two days previous (*HC* 2:335). The Prophet, in attendance at a session of William's debating school, had corrected William on his impatient behavior that evening. The somewhat impetuous younger brother took exception to that. The prophet replied to William's apology with: "However hasty and harsh I may have spoken at any time to you, it has been done for the express purpose of endeavoring to warn, exhort, admonish, and rescue you from falling into difficulties and sorrows . . ." (*HC* 2:342).

"I frequently rebuke and admonish my brethren, and that because I love them, not because I wish to incur their displeasure, or mar their happiness."

(Joseph Smith, *HC* 2:478)

DECEMBER 19

Pliability

Sunday, 19 Dec. 1841: This evening the Twelve meet in session with the Prophet Joseph Smith at his home in Nauvoo. Heber C. Kimball gives a sermon about the parable of the potter, from Jeremiah 18, and concludes, "All that are pliable in the hands of God and are obedient to His commands, are vessels of honor, and God will receive them" (*HC* 4:478). Then, as reported by Wilford Woodruff, the Prophet arises and expands on this theme by stating, "Some people say I am a fallen Prophet, because I do not bring forth more of the word of the Lord. Why do I not do it? Are we able to receive it? No! not one in this room" (*HC* 4:478). He then chastened the congregation for their wickedness and unbelief, "for whom the Lord loveth he chasteneth, and scourgeth every son and daughter whom he receiveth" (*HC* 4:478–479). Pliability is humbly accepting the commandments and chastisements of the Lord.

DECEMBER 20
Death of the Faithful

Tuesday, 20 Dec. 1842: "Elder Lorenzo D. Barnes died this morning at a quarter past three o'clock, at Bradford England. He is the first Elder who has fallen in a foreign land in these last days. He had been long connected with the Church, and had been distinguished, both in his native land and in Great Britain, for his piety, and virtue" (*HC* 5:207). In a subsequent eulogy for Brother Barnes, who had succumbed unexpectedly to a severe fever, Elder Parley P. Pratt said: "Brother Barnes was everywhere known and universally beloved as a meek, humble, and zealous minister of the Gospel, who has labored extensively for many years with great success. Such was his wisdom and prudence, and such his modesty and kindness, that he won the friendship not only of the Saints, but of thousands of various sects . . . His name and memory . . . will be handed down to all generations, as one who has . . . laid down his life for Christ's sake and the Gospel's, to find it again, even life eternal" (*HC* 5:319–320).

DECEMBER 21
Scripture Study

Monday, 21 Dec. 1835: "Spent this day at home, endeavoring to treasure up knowledge for the benefit of my calling" (*HC* 2:344). The outcome of the Prophet's devoted study is clear: "The day passed off very pleasantly. I thank the Lord for His blessings to my soul, His great mercy over my family in sparing our lives. O continue Thy care over me and mine, for Christ's sake" (*HC* 2:344). His studies and contemplation, no doubt of the word of God, increased his acknowledgement of God's mercy and protecting care, his prayerfulness, and his Christ-centered humility. Thus we catch a private glimpse of a prophet of God's constant preparation to carry out the errand of the Lord.

"I find that when I get casual in my relationship with divinity and when it seems that no divine ear is listening and no divine voice is speaking, that I am far, far away. If I immerse myself in the scriptures the distance narrows and the spirituality returns. . . . [No one] should get so busy that he or she does not have time to study the scriptures and the words of modern prophets."

(Spencer W. Kimball, *The Teachings of Spencer W. Kimball*, 135–136)

DECEMBER 22
Proclamation

Wednesday, 22 Dec. 1841: The Prophet Joseph Smith writes: "This evening I commenced giving instructions to the scribe concerning writing the proclamation to the kings of the earth, mentioned in the revelation given January 19, 1841" (*HC* 4:483–484). The Prophet refers to Section 124: "This proclamation shall be made to all the kings of the world . . . and the high-minded governors of the nation in which you live, and to all the nations of the earth scattered abroad" (v. 3; see also D&C 1:23). Thus the Lord would call on the nations to "give heed to the light and glory of Zion" (v. 6), to repent, and to use their resources and influence to support the building up of the kingdom of God. This gospel pattern of warning all nations is continued in our day, such as with "The Family: A Proclamation to the World."

"To the rulers and people of all nations, we solemnly declare again that. . . . The great and dreadful day of the Lord is near at hand. . . . Turn unto the Lord, seek his forgiveness, and unite yourselves in humility with his kingdom."

(Ezra Taft Benson, *Ensign,* Nov. 1975, 33–34)

DECEMBER 23

The Prophet Joseph Smith

Monday, 23 Dec. 1805: Joseph Smith is born in Sharon township, Windsor County, Vermont, to Joseph Smith, Sr., schoolteacher and farmer, and Lucy Mack Smith. By naming him Joseph, the parents were fulfilling ancient prophecy; by bringing the boy forth in the latter days, the Lord was enacting the plan laid down before the foundation of the world, whereby He would restore again His gospel. Only 39 short years would pass before Joseph's great work would be done and the foundation put in place. John Taylor of the Twelve, an eyewitness of the martyrdom of Joseph and Hyrum, would then proclaim that "in the short space of twenty years . . . Joseph Smith, the Prophet and Seer of the Lord, has done more, save Jesus only, for the salvation of men in this world, than any other man that ever lived in it" (D&C 135:3).

"As latter-day Saints who have this testimony of [Joseph Smith's] mission, we should never allow his birthday to pass without thanking God for the inspiration of that man."

(Heber J. Grant, *Liahona: The Elders' Journal,* 21:237)

DECEMBER 24

Courage

Sunday, 24 Dec. 1837: This day marks the marriage of Hyrum Smith and Mary Fielding in Kirtland, Ohio. Few women of the Restoration epitomize courage and valor in a more exemplary way than this remarkable young Canadian convert. She became the mother of Joseph F. Smith, sixth President of the Church, and the grandmother of Joseph Fielding Smith, tenth President of the Church. Following the martyrdom of Hyrum and Joseph, Mary Fielding and her widowed sister, Mercy, nurtured and cared for their two families with angelic compassion and fortitude as they prepared for the daunting exodus to the West. Mary's inspiring motto—"The Lord will open the way"—rallied her children to action in the face of overwhelming challenges (see *Teachings of Presidents of the Church: Joseph F. Smith*, xiv).

"We too can develop the virtue of courage in our own lives. . . . Indeed, 'God hath not given us the spirit of fear; but of power, and of love, and of a sound mind' (2 Tim. 1:7)."

(Susan Easton Black, *Ensign*, Mar. 1997, 51)

DECEMBER 25

Listening

Tuesday, 25 Dec. 1832: On Christmas Day, the day of peace, the Prophet Joseph Smith receives what he terms a "revelation and a prophecy on war" (Section 87; see *HC* 1:301–302). Though a number of prominent thinkers of the day were persuaded that conflict between the North and South might well unfold, the Prophet, through inspiration, predicts with astounding accuracy the salient details of the coming Civil War and future conflicts. From this we learn that the Lord presides over the sweep of history, and that He will guide His Saints, through the prophets, to refuge in holy places if they are obedient. In all dispensations, those who heed the counsel of prophets have found a measure of safety and peace.

"'And the voice of warning shall be unto all people, by the mouths of my disciples, whom I have chosen in these last days' (D&C 1:1–3). God has solutions! There is only one real road to safety and that is to hearken unto the voice of the prophet of God."

(Hartman Rector Jr., *Ensign,* Nov. 1975, 10–11)

DECEMBER 26
Forgiveness

Saturday, 26 Dec. 1835: The Prophet records: "Brother Lyman Sherman came in, and requested to have the word of the Lord through me; 'for,' said he, 'I have been wrought upon to make known to you my feelings and desires, and was promised that I should have a revelation which should make known my duty'" (*HC* 2:345). In response, the Lord gives Section 108, which begins: "Verily thus saith the Lord unto you, my servant Lyman: Your sins are forgiven you, because you have obeyed my voice in coming up hither this morning to receive counsel of him whom I have appointed. Therefore, let your soul be at rest concerning your spiritual standing, and resist no more my voice. And arise up and be more careful henceforth in observing your vows, which you have made and do make, and you shall be blessed with exceeding great blessings" (D&C 108:1–3).

"In all our forgiving and seeking forgiveness, we must recognize that. . . . it is in Christ that 'we have redemption through his blood, the forgiveness of sins, according to the riches of his grace' (Eph. 1:7)."

(Cecil O. Samuelson Jr., *Ensign,* Feb. 2003, 51)

DECEMBER 27
Peace

Thursday, 27 Dec. 1832: On this day (and the next) the Prophet Joseph Smith receives Section 88 (vv. 1–126, the remainder coming on January 3, 1833). This material is characterized by the Prophet in a letter to W.W. Phelps as follows: "I send you the 'olive leaf' which we have plucked from the Tree of Paradise, the Lord's message of peace to us" (*HC* 1:316). And a magnificent gift of peace it is, for this marvelous revelation outlines in comprehensive detail principles upon which the Saints may obtain peace, such as receiving light and truth, obeying celestial law, and sanctifying themselves—all resulting in eventual redemption of the soul and its consignment to a sphere of glory.

"The famed statesman, William Gladstone, described the formula for peace when he declared: 'We look forward to the time when the power of love will replace the love of power. Then will our world know the blessings of peace.' World peace, though a lofty goal, is but an outgrowth of the personal peace each individual seeks to attain. I speak not of the peace promoted by man, but peace as promised of God."

(Thomas S. Monson, *Ensign,* May 1994, 61)

DECEMBER 28
Charity in Temple Work

Tuesday, 28 Dec. 1841: The Prophet's entry is short, but interesting: "I baptized Sidney Rigdon in the font, for and in behalf of his parents; also baptized Reynolds Cahoon and others" (*HC* 4:486). The baptismal font of the Nauvoo Temple had been dedicated by Brigham Young a month previous. The Prophet captures the essence of this sacred work during a sermon he delivered on May 12, 1844, just a few weeks before his martyrdom: "Every man that has been baptized and belongs to the kingdom has a right to be baptized for those who have gone before . . . for those whom we have much friendship for" (*HC* 6:365–366).

"The ideals of faith, hope, and charity are most evident in the holy temples. . . . Performing temple ordinances for the dead is a manifestation of charity, offering essential blessings to those who have preceded us, blessings that were not available to them during their mortal lives. We have the privilege of doing for them what they are unable to do for themselves."

(Joseph B. Wirthlin, *Ensign,* Nov. 1998, 27)

DECEMBER 29
Bold Speaking with Inspiration

Thursday, 29 Dec. 1842: Joseph Smith recalls on this extremely cold winter day a similar day in Missouri when the tavern owners had refused his company refuge from the elements: "Such was the extreme cold that in one hour we must have perished. We pleaded for our women and children in vain. We counseled together, and the brethren agreed to stand by me, and we concluded that we might as well die fighting as to freeze to death" (*HC* 5:211). When the landlord again refuses to give them lodging, citing rumors that the Mormons were "very bad people," the Prophet steps forward in power. "I said to him, 'We will stay; but no thanks to you. I have men enough to take the town; and if we must freeze, we will freeze by the burning of these houses.' The taverns were then opened, and we were accommodated, and received many apologies in the morning from the inhabitants for their abusive treatment" (*HC* 5:211). The Prophet followed the promptings of the Spirit to take charge of a challenging situation and preserve the well-being of his people, using speech he might not have considered otherwise.

DECEMBER 30
Patience

Wednesday, 30 Dec. 1840: Joseph receives a letter from Brigham Young in Liverpool giving a glowing report of the growth of the Church in England: "I pray the Lord to roll on His work in that great city [London]," writes Brigham Young (*HC* 4:251). The Apostle then concludes his letter in a unique way: "I am as ever, your brother in the Kingdom of Patience, Brigham Young." What better description could there be for the kingdom of God—particularly in its missionary phase—than to call it the "Kingdom of Patience"?

"When we are unduly impatient, however, we are, in effect, trying to hasten an outcome when acceleration would abuse agency. Enoch, brilliant, submissive, and spiritual, knew what it meant to see a whole city-culture advance in "process of time." He could tell us so much about so many things, including patience. . . . Patience is a willingness, in a sense, to watch the unfolding purposes of God with a sense of wonder and awe—rather than pacing up and down within the cell of our circumstance."

(Neal A. Maxwell, *Ensign*, Oct. 1980, 28–29)

DECEMBER 31
Hope

Monday, 31 Dec. 1838: The close of the year 1838 finds the Prophet Joseph Smith and his colleagues incarcerated in Liberty Jail. Here they have been languishing in squalor for a full month. The Prophet's final words for the year are as follows: "We were sometimes visited by our friends, whose kindness and attention I shall ever remember with feelings of lively gratitude; but frequently we were not suffered to have that privilege. Our food was of the coarsest kind, and served up in a manner which was disgusting. Thus, in a land of liberty, in the town of Liberty, Clay County, Missouri, my fellow prisoners and I in chains, and dungeons, saw the close of 1838" (*HC* 3:244). And yet the coming of the New Year evokes stoically positive sentiments from the Prophet: "The day dawned upon us as prisoners of hope, but not as sons of liberty" (*HC* 3:245).

"Unsurprisingly the triad of faith, hope, and charity, which brings us to Christ, has strong and converging linkage (see Ether 12:28; Moro. 7:47)."

(Neal A. Maxwell, *Ensign*, Nov. 1994, 35.)

Index to Themes

ED J. PINEGAR

Brother Pinegar is a retired dentist and a long-time teacher of early-morning seminary and religion classes at Brigham Young University. He teaches at the Joseph Smith Academy and has served as a mission president in England and at the Missionary Training Center in Provo, Utah. He has been a bishop twice, a stake president, and is a temple sealer. Brother Pinegar and his wife Patricia are the parents of eight children, and reside in Orem, Utah.

RICHARD J. ALLEN

Richard J. Allen is a husband, father, teacher, writer, and organizational consultant. He has served on several stake high councils, in several stake presidencies, and as a bishop. Brother Allen has filled many teaching assignments in the Church, including being a full-time missionary, a gospel doctrine teacher, and a stake institute instructor. He has served as a faculty member at both Brigham Young University and The Johns Hopkins University. Richard has authored or co-authored many articles, manuals, and books, and loves to study the scriptures and Church history. He and his wife Carol Lynn have four children and live in Orem, Utah.

PAUL A. JENSEN

Paul A. Jensen served a mission in Norway, and has since served on several high councils and bishoprics. He attended Brigham Young University and several other universities, and is a respected and successful businessman in Utah and other areas. He is also a former seminary teacher. Paul is currently the CEO of the Mrs. Cavanaugh's chain of stores. He and his wife Jennifer live in Sandy, Utah.